THE STORY OF
ST KATHARINE'S

———◦———

I dedicate my book to Oskar, Lola, Natasha, Florence and Hector.

Within this story are examples of beauty, brilliance, excellence and success, as well as dishonesty, failure, incompetence, stupidity and worse; it's for you and today's other young people to shape the future.

THE STORY OF
ST KATHARINE'S

Christopher West

THE CLOISTER HOUSE PRESS

First published in the United Kingdom in 2014 by
The Cloister House Press

ISBN 978-1-909465-25-1

Contents

————◅◦▻————

Introduction

———◁◦▷———

Living close to St Katharine Docks has become a love story. From the first day I adored the nearness of the Thames, witness to our history down the ages, the inspiration offered by Tower Bridge and the elegance and vibrancy of the Marina. Does any other community have a more interesting set of neighbours than Wapping and the Tower of London? I then heard about the ancient Royal Hospital and Church, here from 1148, and the old ways of nearby London Docks and its dockers, which led me to wonder how St Katharine Docks came about. I recalled visiting forty years ago – how did it transform into what it is today? Finding these answers was fascinating, and so I decided to write it all down, simply because no one else had done so. I have done my amateur best to tell the story. Be patient with any errors – I have made serious effort to check and double check facts, and to attribute sources correctly. I chose to write independently, without favour or influence from others, some of whom may have more knowledge and insight than me; so the observations and views presented are strictly my own, following careful listening (and reading) to a wide range of views. The book is intended as a light read and my two desires are to offer a record and stimulate thought for those who may wish to follow in greater detail – there are three big subjects each worthy of a further book. Please do contact me with comments, observations and criticism – I will be pleased to offer further information in any way practicable via thestoryofstk@outlook.com.

Particular thanks to Michelle Anderson for her extensive proofreading and 'book support' skills; Jane Young (good advice and excellent sketches), Kate Taylor (editing and early support), Christopher Adach (many of the best photographs), Miles Bailey and the team at The Choir Press (excellent advice, tact and organisation), Brian Heyte, who has very sadly died (advice and wealth of local knowledge), Dock owners Max Property Group giving permission for photography, Adèle Haselgrove (extensive advice), Camilla (always encouraging and helpful), Neil Turner (advice about South Quay), my dear old computer and windows 97, without which I would still be writing. Thanks to many friends for encouragement and to numerous sources who have let me see confidential documents for 'information and own use only'. Humblest apology to anyone overlooked.

CHAPTER ONE

A History of the Royal Hospital of St Katharine by The Tower

————◄○►————

The Early Hospital Tradition

The word 'hospital' comes from the Latin hospes, meaning stranger or guest. In Mediaeval times travellers and pilgrims would be fed and housed in monasteries while travelling and visiting various holy places around Europe and the Middle East. As these journeys would have been arduous, often lengthy and dangerous, they would require time to recover and rest. This developed the need for more space and beds; being Christian organisations, these people needed to be administered to bodily as well as spiritually, and so hospitals gradually developed separately to monasteries. Sick people who may not have been able to continue travelling would hence become members of the community, and those that died would need burying. Education became important in hospitals, not least because pregnant women often lost husbands and thus would need looking after with their children; schools were therefore needed and the pupils often attended church as choristers. These buildings were usually developed as a large hall joined to a smaller structure, which would serve as a church. St Bartholomew's is the oldest hospital in London, founded in 1123 under the auspices of the Augustinian St Bartholomew's Priory in West Smithfield. Eastwards and closer to the Thames lay the Augustinian Priory of Holy Trinity, who would also have felt the same need for offering better accommodation for travellers.

Tenth Century

King Edgar gave thirteen acres of land to a group of knights, who hence founded a 'Knighten Guild' on land now referred to as St Katharine's, building up extensive trade in the area.

Twelfth Century

Queen Matilda

1125: The descendants of this land donated it to the Holy Trinity, an Augustinian Priory in nearby Aldgate. 1148 (approx): Queen Matilda of Boulogne (wife of King Stephen) founded the Hospital of St Katharine by the Tower.

Master's Staff, RFSK

Royal Hospital of St Katharine

Matilda, the foundress, created and endowed her foundation
to benefit her own soul and those of King Stephen and their
children, including two sons, Eustace and William, who died
as infants and were buried in the Priory Church of Holy
Trinity at Aldgate. The governance of the hospital was laid
down by Queen Matilda to maintain a chapter of four
brethren, one of whom would be in charge, three sisters, six
'poor clerks' and certain other poor persons. Interestingly, the
sisters were given equal status to the brothers, involving
considerable authority. The term Master evolved for the
leader, though he required the votes in chapter for matters of
importance. Two of the prime duties of the Hospital were to
regularly celebrate Mass, in particular for the souls as laid
down in the Queen's charter, and to serve the poor and infirm
people in the Hospital. The Augustinian Priory of Holy Trinity,
Aldgate, also owned the land on which the later Royal College
of St Katharine was formed at Poplar, after its return to the
East End.

St Katharine, at her current home at the RFSK, Limehouse

The legend of St Katharine (or Catherine) of Alexandria was popular and well known around England during the eleventh century; she lived in Alexandria in the fourth century, her feast day is November 25th and she is the patron saint of philosophers and preachers. Born of a noble family, she converted to Christianity and denounced King Maxentius for persecuting Christians, before eventually being imprisoned and condemned to death – her limbs were broken on a spoked wheel, which then broke, so she was killed by beheading. Her voice is said to have been one of those heard by St Joan of Arc. It may be that the suggested name came from Queen Matilda herself, or from the Priory, which already administered St Katharine Coleman (in Magpie Alley, Fenchurch Street) and St Katharine Cree (Leadenhall Street). The early hospital was built from west to east, probably as a large rectangular hall with a church (or chapel) adjoining it, separated by a screen.

1190: The Precinct lost land to the Tower, which needed to strengthen its fortifications by building a stone wall and moat; this included the mill granted by Queen Matilda, other properties and a garden. Compensation was not finally settled until fifty years later, under King Edward I.

Thirteenth Century

By the 1250s a serious rift had developed between the Hospital and the Priory. The Brothers were said to have become ill disciplined and subject to alcohol abuse and serious infighting. One of the Prior's canons was placed in the

Madonna and Jesus icon, now at RFSK at Limehouse

Hospital to put matters right, but incensed by this, the Brothers took legal action against the Prior, which culminated in an enquiry by the Mayor Of London (being the King's representative for the area) and a jury of aldermen, rather than ordinary citizens, probably because of the Prior's own rank of alderman. Judgement was given against the Brothers, strengthening the authority of the Prior. The struggle continued as the Chapter appealed to Queen Eleanor with various complaints against the Prior and the Canon (still installed at the Hospital). The dispute continued with correspondence from the Prior to the Pope and the Queen to the Bishop of London, but the problems were finally settled and from 1261 onwards St Katharine's was destined to be under the definite patronage of the Queens of England, right up to the present day. (Footnote: a fully researched, detailed account of this and many other issues is given in Catherine

Jamison's scholarly book, 'The History of The Royal Hospital Of St Katharine By The Tower of London'). At various times in the future, pressure was applied to increase influence or control at the Hospital, but would be successfully resisted owing to the precedent set by Queen Eleanor and her predecessor, Queen Matilda. During this period, various properties and land were given by the Queen and others, adding to the income of the Hospital.

On the 5th July 1273 Queen Eleanor granted a new charter consolidating and increasing expectations laid down by Queen Matilda. Her husband, King Henry III, had since died and Eleanor decreed that Mass should be said daily for his soul and the souls of all past kings and queens. She laid down some changes in organisation, addressed issues of increase in size and decreed that only she and her successors could appoint the Master, Brethren and Sisters, or change the articles of the charter. This charter was confirmed by her son, Edward I, in 1292 and later by her grandson, Edward II, in 1317. Various criticisms were made about unclear aspects of the charter, giving rise to numerous legal challenges in the future, as well as financial difficulties due to underfunding as the Hospital's obligations and community numbers increased.

Thomas Leckelade, commissioned by Queen Eleanor, resigned as Master during 1293 after approximately twenty years; he was succeeded by Walter Redinges in the same year, by order of King Henry I. After a few years various complaints were made, not least by the Brothers and Sisters, claiming that the Hospital had become dilapidated. Whether because Redinges was a poor administrator, was taking funds for himself, or both, in 1299 the King ordered an audit of the Hospitals affairs, followed a year later by a formal visitation.

In the year that followed the Hospital faced further financial problems when demands were made from the Exchequer for a sum of money owed from the lands gifted by Queen Eleanor. Fortunately, the King swiftly ordered the barons of the Exchequer to withhold their demands, and St Katharine's was given a discharge.

Fourteenth Century

In 1333 Queen Philippa's power was put to the test and upheld. Richard de Lusteshull (Master from 1318) had been appointed by Queen Isabella, but dismissed for squandering goods belonging to the Hospital, and Queen Philippa gave the post to Roger Bast. Lusteshull took his case to Parliament and the king in 1333, to be told that it would proceed to trial. Queen Philippa, however, argued that by the terms of the Foundation's Charter the judges would not have jurisdiction, and the King decided that the matter should rest with the Queen and Her council. In 1338 fund raising for the rebuilding of the church was begun by William de Kildesby (Master from 1338/39 and previously the Queens treasurer).

In 1350 Queen Philippa founded a chantry in the Hospital and provided funding for an additional chaplain by gifted lands yielding £10 per year.

By 1351 discipline was problematical again, so to assist the Master, the Queen issued a document now referred to as Queen Philippa's Ordinances, which gave a code of conduct for behaviour and expectation of the Brethren. Foremost, she endorsed all the directives laid down by Queen Matilda, there would be a Master (warden or keeper), three Brothers and three Sisters who would be holy and virtuous, performing divine service daily in the church of the Hospital, assisted by three or more poor scholars. Some of the main rules included that the brothers and sisters were to have no private property except with the agreement of the Master, they should not go out without his consent, nor stay out after curfew. The Sisters were allowed 20 shillings per annum for clothing, the Brothers 40 shillings. The habit was to be black, worn with a cloak with the sign of St. Katharine, and the wearing of green or red clothes was prohibited; the Brothers were to have no private conference with the Sisters or any other women; negligence or disobedience on the part of the Brothers and Sisters was punishable by lessening their portion of food and drink but not by stripes (beating); each Sister was to eat in her room; her daily allowance was a white and a brown loaf, two pieces of different kinds of meat value 1 1/2d, or fish of the same value, and a pittance (extra money for food or wine on special occasions, such as a religious festival or anniversary of a benefactor) worth 1d.; the portion of both Brothers and Sisters was to be doubled on fifteen feast days; the Master was to dine in the common hall with the Brothers; the almswomen were to wear caps and cloaks of a grey colour; they were not to go out without leave of the Master; if their conduct was bad they could be removed by the Master with consent of the Brothers and Sisters. Other ordinances concerned the care of the sick and the transaction of business relating to the properties belonging to the Hospital. Some provision was made for funding, though inadequate for all that was expected of the institution, particularly as it became bigger.

Problems continued, though records show that by 1368 the new Master, John de Hermesthorpe, was proving to be very effective. His involvement spanned more than 40 years, until his death, during which time his administration skills and dedication led to much improvement and enhancement of the Hospital's reputation. By 1377 the nave had been finished and the mills belonging to the church had been rebuilt; the Master had contributed £2000 of his own money for this. The Church's wooden choir stalls, with elaborate and ornate carvings, became famous and were probably installed during this period; though they were skilfully removed when the Church was destroyed and may still be seen today at the Royal Foundation at Poplar; most remarkable are those created for the Master, Brethren and Sisters.

Queen Philippa died in 1369, and in 1376 Edward II decreed an annual grant of £10 per year for a chaplain to daily celebrate mass in the chantry founded by her. He also endowed Rushingdon Manor on the Isle of Sheppey, 60 acres of pasture and 120 acres of salt marsh in the parish of Minster to provide funds for another chaplain.

In 1377 a visitation was made by Chancellor Adam Houghton, Bishop of St David's, assisted by the Clerk of the

Rolls of Chancery, the Archdeacon of Lincoln and three clerks of the Chancery. Master Hermesthorpe, attended by his three Brothers and three Sisters, appeared for questioning and the reported findings were very positive; the services impressed as devoutly performed and proper discipline was being maintained. It was also found that income was seriously insufficient for the number of duties ordered. Then, in 1380, a goldsmith called John de Chichester bequeathed lands and property to establish another chantry, and was followed by several others, carefully encouraged, no doubt, by the Master. In 1386 he successfully removed numerous dubious inhabitants from properties owned in East Smithfield. John de Hermesthorpe

Ornately carved entrance doors, Master's and Chapter stalls, orginally from the west wall of the Hospital, installed late 14th century. Now in use at RFSK Limehouse, remarkably well preserved.

remained Master right up to his death in 1412, having successfully exploited the adjacent land to attract good quality neighbours, substantially improving the buildings and the Hospital's income. By the late 1300s, the area was referred to as the Liberty or Precinct of St Katharine's. In his will he directed that he should be buried in the choir of the Church, in front of the image of St Katharine, and left all his money to be shared out among the people at the Hospital.

Fifteenth Century

In 1438 King Henry VI appointed his secretary, Thomas Bekington, to be Master. Like Hermesthorpe before him, he worked energetically to improve the Hospital's position and efficiency and was generous in his will after his death, twenty years later. At his request the King granted a new charter of privileges in 1441/2, which significantly altered its status and was necessary because the Hospital was still struggling to finance itself. The charter provided for the Hospital and the inhabitants of the Precinct to be for the most part independent, subject only to the jurisdiction of the Chancellor of England and the Master or his deputy. Its own court and prison was built and further officers were appointed. Most importantly, the

More fine wood carvings, known as misericords, at RFSK Limehouse

Brothers' houses

Precinct was now removed from the authority of the City of London, which allowed commerce, trade and industry to flourish in the wharves and docks, and must have been a constant source of annoyance down the centuries to the Mayor, aldermen and City liveries, who jealously guarded their rights and traditions. The parochial ties with St Botolph without Aldgate were severed, so creating the Hospital Church as the 'parish church' for the inhabitants in all but name.

Sixteenth Century

With the accession of Henry VIII to the throne in 1509, his first wife, Catherine of Aragon, appointed one of her Spanish priests, George de Athequa to the Mastership. A year later the King and Queen founded the Guild (fraternity) of St Barbara, which included other Royals, Cardinal Wolsey and senior Nobles. Some historians argue that Henry's second wife, Anne Boleyn, influenced the King in favour of avoiding dissolution of the Hospital at a time when most religious establishments were being suppressed; it is true that they had often visited the Hospital as a couple, though she was not appointed Patron during the three years that she was Queen. There are several other possible reasons – the independence of the Hospital, thanks to the Charter of 1441/2, the willingness of the incumbents to embrace doctrinal changes and maybe King Henry's own personal attachment. So it survived unscathed, though some changes were made to its provisions and charters. In 1537 Queen Jane Seymour appointed Gilbert Lathom as Master, a good administrator who continued building up the parochial work of the Hospital. In 1541 St Katharine Stairs, which was an important landing stage for the area, was leased (together with the nearby wharf); these Thames access points were important because fees were charged for boats to land and for cargo and passengers' use. The lease allowed free carriage and wharfage use for the Master, Brothers and Sisters, as well as certain rights for the Bedeswomen and other tenants of the Hospital. The Precinct had its own gaol, known as The Hole, which at this period was in Thames Street, near the entrance to St Katharine's Court. King Henry VIII died in 1547, outlived by his last wife, Katherine Parr, who appointed Sir Thomas Seymour as Master. She also married him shortly after Henry's death. He was the first lay Master, breaking the old order of ordained clergy, and unfortunately it was in his period and that of his successor that most of the artefacts and items of value were removed; this included wall hangings, plate and historical artefacts. Seymour's end was inglorious – he was found guilty of treason and beheaded in 1549. Sir Francis Fleming was the next Master, and the Hospital continued from bad to worse. Queen Mary was enthroned in 1553 and undid some of the policies of the previous protestant government; she was unable to reinstall losses (particularly land) to the monasteries, but did set about using her authority as patron to restore the old order to St Katharine's. In 1554 she appointed Francis Mallet as Master, who reintroduced the Latin Mass, spent a great deal on repairs, replaced furniture and created a choir. However, it was unlikely that he was considered well by the incumbents and the people of the Precinct. By 1566 most of the removed valuables were returned – they had probably been stored in the nearby Tower of London. Queen Elizabeth I and her advisers came up with a scheme to put the Hospital under the authority of the Lieutenant of the Tower; this was never enacted, again leaving the Hospital free of authority except by its patron.

During Queen Elizabeth's reign many poor Flemings resided in the Precinct, so the Queen appropriated an area to be called the Flemings Churchyard for their burials, also for other poor residents in this part of the Precinct. A number of Jews also lived near here, at a place called Judaismus.

In 1559 a new religious settlement was made, which reinforced the separation from the Pope in Rome and ended the strong Protestantism which had been developing during the reign of Elizabeth's predecessor, Edward VI. With the resignation of Doctor Mallet in 1561, Queen Elizabeth immediately appointed her secretary Dr Thomas Wilson as Master. Dr Wilson was a lawyer, the first of four to be appointed as Master, and used his skills to disentangle the Hospital from paying ecclesiastical taxes owing to it having been wrongly assessed as a 'College' in the past. He was less successful in attempts to sell off the rights of the Hospital to the City, gained in the charter of 1441/2, which was always keen to gain power over the area and pay a fine price in return – the local residents of the Precinct were furious at this threat to their freedom and restrictions for trade and sent a petition to Sir William Cecil, the Chief Secretary of State. They had very strong arguments because they were also protected as beneficiaries in the charter, it would also cause much damage to livings and trade, be an affront to the authority of the Queen and change three hundred years of direct rule. The Queen and her Council refused to ratify the plan, so Dr Wilson's proposal failed. Nevertheless, he did succeed in raising several hundred pounds by selling off the right given in the 1440s to hold an annual St James' Fair, to the Corporation of London. The custom of the Master giving travellers and poor people hospitality at his table was discontinued as a regular occurrence and Wilson dissolved The Choir, which had achieved very high standards and had been considered, by at least one historian, to be 'not much inferior to that of St Paul's'. He was succeeded by David Lewes, followed by Sir Ralph Rokeby, both Masters of Requests (very senior judges). By act of Parliament in 1572 the first Poor Law made provision for the punishment of sturdy (dangerous) beggars and for the relief of the impotent (respectable) poor; for the Precinct, this meant employing a new group of administrators who developed a system of levying money from the residents for distribution to the needy.

By the 1570s various foreign Nationalities were represented, particularly Dutch and French. In 1589 the two docks (St Katharine's and Seggie Dock) were leased for 80 years – during this period part of the main dock became a wharf and Seggie was filled in, then built upon with houses. Fuel, including coal and wood import, was an important trade and there was a prosperous glassworks; Flemish brewers built several breweries, creating a lasting tradition for the area. One particular brewer was twice in trouble with the authorities, firstly for exporting too much and secondly for watering down the beer. At this time building new houses was developing apace and Rokeby encouraged this further, continuing the custom of the Hospital being the freeholder. From 1598 records show the use of constables (appointed by the Master) for policing the Precinct. Similarly, Scavengers were appointed to serve for a year, to collect a rate from residents which paid for the rakers, whose job was to remove rubbish and filth from the streets; they also ensured that residents paved the frontage of their houses and kept their immediate surround clear of rubbish – failure was reported to the constable. This job was lowly and unpopular, but was considered as a first step up the ladder for those interested in becoming officials or officers. For this purpose, there were two wards, upper and lower, with two scavengers for each ward. Plagues were relatively well organised in the Precinct – records show that the death rate during the Great Plague of 1665 was approximately half that of areas close by.

Some time before Rokeby's death in 1596, Dr Julius Caesar,

Sir Julius Caesar, Master

the son of an Italian immigrant (related to the Duke of Cesarini, hence the name) who had been involved with the Hospital for some years, had managed to obtain what has been described as 'the reversion of the Mastership', purchased for £500, paid to the Scottish ambassador. Queen Elizabeth was very displeased, but here continued an important part of the Hospital's history. Dr Caesar's father had built up a considerable medical practice, also acting as physician to both Queen Mary and Elizabeth, accumulating considerable wealth in the process. Julius trained as a lawyer and his association began under the mastership of Dr Lewes, who had appointed him chancellor of the ecclesiastical Court in 1581, during which time he built up a reputation as a fair and impartial judge; the main issues before this court were probate of wills and marital disputes, with many other crimes, such as witchcraft, heresy, fornication and defamation. He retained that position until Rokeby's death, after which he became Master, and brought his family to live with him. He had obtained a doctorate of Canon Law in 1684, become MP for Windsor and was reappointed as Master in 1603; in the same year he was knighted by King James at Greenwich. He later became MP for Middlesex, then Maldon.

Seventeenth Century

By now Sir Julius Caesar had also achieved the post as Chancellor of the Exchequer and Privy Council member. His role as Master lasted forty years. He was a good administrator and very active within the Precinct and introduced various reforms. Three of his sons and one grandson held office within the Precinct. He was generous with money from his own purse in the purchase of large amounts of furniture and money for repairs and upkeep, and commissioned a carved pulpit, which is still used (and well preserved) at the Royal Foundation of St Katharine at Limehouse. In 1614 he was appointed as Master of the Rolls (the second most senior judge in the country, under the Lord Chief Justice) which office he held until his death in 1636. Leaving substantial amounts to the Brethren, he was buried at St Helen's, Bish-

Sir Julius Caesar's pulpit

opsgate. The Precinct was further expanding; a soap making factory was built in the 1630s, adding to the numbers of tradesmen needed for employment; by now there was also a considerable number of residents employed in the professions, including doctors and lawyers, as well as many officials and officers employed at the nearby Tower of London. Henry Montague became the next Master and survived in post throughout the Civil War of 1642 – 1651; his brother was the 2nd Earl of Manchester, who served as a general in Cromwell's army. In 1653 he left the post – there were various criticisms about the standards pertaining at the time. In 1651 the constables engaged eight watchmen for night duty; two at the Iron Gate, two at the Dock and four at St Katharine Stairs. The successful control of disease was partly due to the great work of the constables. A system had evolved whereby, during periods of plague, officers involved in collecting for the poor also had the task of collecting for the sick – they distributed the collection to these people, who were then strictly confined to their houses and guarded by neighbours who were paid to ensure that the sick person didn't break this method of quarantine; this was overseen strictly by the constables. The relative cleanliness of the area is likely to be the other reason, thanks to the work of the scavengers and rakers.

In 1672 there was a terrible fire in which a hundred houses were destroyed. Eventually, Montague's half brother, George, was appointed as Master and remained in post until his death, in 1681. Sadly, from the 1660s to the end of the century, further decline continued because of a series of disputes about who should be Master, letting of properties and claims and counter claims involving authority of the patrons. The Masters who were appointed were of little use, so without proper management and upkeep of the buildings they further dilapidated, and the pressures and hardship suffered by the Brethren and poor people in the Precinct must have been awful. Numerous attempts were made by the Brothers, Sisters and bedeswomen to get help, but without good leadership their efforts fell on deaf ears. The trend was reported as similar to other Royal Hospitals and churches in the country at this period, verging on disgraceful and notorious. At last, in 1696, two of the Brothers and the Sisters succeeded in persuading the Attorney General to bring a Chancery suit against Sir James Butler, who had been appointed Master in 1664 – arguments followed whether the Chancery Court had jurisdiction, so no action appears to have been taken by Judge Sir John Somers, who heard the case, but it did lead to a commission, chaired by the same Judge, to visit the Hospital, with the full powers for investigation given by the patron. In the interim, Sir James Butler was appointed Lord Chancellor. Following this extensive visitation, the findings were published, which condemned the Master's conduct and vindicated the various demands which had repeatedly been requested. The conditions at the Hospital were seriously criticised, rent revenues had been kept for the personal use of the Master, who had greatly usurped his authority and disabused the rights of the Brethren in chapter, as well as having treated them without respect and courtesy. Sir James Butler was deprived of his Mastership and made to pay £1000 in costs, several others were suspended or dismissed. The Lord Chancellor then issued guidelines for the better government of the Hospital, which recommended financial procedures that would put its finances on a proper businesslike basis for the first time in its history, giving proper guidelines to prevent future maladministration or improper use by future Masters. Furthermore, the chapter was to meet regularly, an original rule that had been allowed to lapse, and a new role of chapter clerk was to be enacted, to oversee the agreement of new leases and enter all chapter records in a register.

Eighteenth Century

In the early 1700s previous schooling in the Precinct was better formalised by the foundation of a Charity School, founded and managed by Trustees chosen by the residents. Fifty children were educated and clothed from this time. By

1705 a new school room had been built over the porch at the west end of the Church. Of prime importance, these children were taught according to the current Church of England constitution and Louis de Durfort, Earl of Faversham, who was appointed Master by the Dowager Queen, to replace the disgraced Sir James Butler, together with the chapter, gave every encouragement and backing to the progress of these children. The main subjects covered were reading, writing and arithmetic/accounts, also singing. The girls were additionally taught house craft and needlework. The students were schooled from the age of eight to fourteen, the boys then moved mainly on to apprenticeships, while the girls were placed in service. In 1792 new, improved school premises were planned by the Chapter, and temporary new accommodation was offered at a house in Queen's Square while a new school was planned to be put in New Street, with a structure to have room for forty boys and twenty girls. Unfortunately, because the Precinct was destroyed in 1825, these plans never materialised.

Louis de Durfort set about enacting the Constitutions laid down by Lord Chancellor Somers. He served nine years, until his death in 1709, during which he was diligent and overall successful in his work to repair the untold damage of the recent past; he regularly attended the chapter meetings, held fortnightly (unless business required more). New leases were negotiated with tenants and the value of the property was generally improved. In 1709 Queen Anne (patron) appointed Dr Henry Newton, previously the English ambassador to Florence, as the new Master; by now the Bedeswomen were receiving their increased pensions and within three years, rental income had considerably increased. Lord Somers' constitutions continued to improve standards, eventually leading to a substantial improvement in the Precinct's finances. William Farrer, a prominent lawyer, succeeded Newton as Master, from 1715 to 1727 and it is understood that the new Sisters appointed were more aristocratic in nature. In 1725 a workhouse was built in Great Garden, designed to provide work for the unemployed. 1734 saw another bad fire, destroying about thirty houses. The 1750s saw the planning of improved buildings under the Mastership of Edmund Waller, appointed in 1747 by King George II. During his forty years as Master he presided over the rebuilding of the Master's house on the North side of the Cloister and the removal of the previously adjoining court house, to be rebuilt on the North side of the Chancel, to adjoin the Chapter house which also served as the Precinct vestry (meeting room). Two of the Brothers houses were also demolished and replaced by three brick houses. Improvements and repair was made to the Sisters and Bedeswomens houses. Improvements were also made to the water inlet from the river. In 1755 Dr Andrew Ducarel, a lawyer, was appointed as an officer in the Ecclesiastical Court; he was a very experienced antiquarian and published the first history of the Hospital, presenting it to Queen Caroline, the then Patron. The work, though valuable for various detail, was incomplete because he was frustrated by the lack of openness from the Chapter, who jealously guarded various historical information and did not allow him proper access to the records. Ducarel was also involved in major work elsewhere, so his time was limited and he was severely handicapped by having the use of only one eye – nevertheless, he was highly respected and gained a strong reputation for integrity and professionalism. Extensive renovations were made to the Church during the 1770s, including the reglazing of the huge east window, which was one of the largest in London, giving unusually good lightness to the Church. New pews were made, paving stones were laid within the alter rails in alternating black and white marble, with steps of Portland stone; a larger gallery was built, to replace the previous one. A new screen, altar-piece and communion table were added, with repairs carried out to the chancel ceiling. By the 1770s the water frontage at St Katharine's was becoming extremely important and valuable, both for international trade and the huge increase in coastal traffic. Iron Gate Wharf became well established and the Chapter actively encouraged extensive development work to the other wharves, with the building of extensive new warehouse accommodation; as old wooden buildings were knocked down, strict attention was paid to the quality of brick replacement buildings, which also cut the number of fires and covenants for ensuring tenants looked after and maintained their properties was greatly modernised.

In 1779 a new organ was purchased. In 1780 the Gordon Riots took place across London and St Katharine's found itself under attack, probably because of its previous association with Popery; the attack was thwarted by the arrival of gentlemen of the London Association. Three ring-leaders were arrested, tried at the Old Bailey and hanged at Tower Hill. By the end of the 1790s, the entire roof and tracery (stonework

Old Church organ

supporting the glass) of the East window were renewed. In 1800 rooms above the porch were removed and the small bell turret was replaced by a bell tower; also, the west front of the Church was restored. In 1771 the Chapter had cause for concern about the future of the Precinct and informed the Patron, Queen Charlotte, accordingly; by 1796 it was known that the City of London was applying for an act of parliament which included a scheme to convert the Precinct into wet docks. It is likely that the Queen defeated the scheme at this stage, giving the Chapter what turned out to be a false sense of security.

Nineteenth Century

In 1818 Major General Sir Herbert Taylor was appointed Master, having previously been private secretary to George III and then the Queen, until her death, also in 1818. As well as now being Master, he resumed his military duties at the same time and became a Member of Parliament (for the City of London) in 1820. The Prince Regent was enthroned as King George IV in the same year and his estranged wife returned to England and was made Patron of St Katharine's. The King issued divorce proceedings, but Queen Charlotte died the following year, having been denied access to his coronation and being allowed to be crowned as Queen. During this time, the British public was deeply split and unhappy about the King's behaviour and immorality. His broken marriage had festered for years, and the Chapter is known to have written an address in support of the Queen, as Patron, expressing their indignation. By 1823 the threat was becoming obvious.

Queen Charlotte

The St Katharine Docks Company, formed by the owners of the London and Victoria and Albert Docks, sought and gained permission, by act of parliament in 1825, to raze the area to the ground and build the docks. The initial St Katharine Dock Company Bill had failed in 1824 (contested fiercely by the London Dock Company) and there was great rejoicing in the streets of the Precinct, but this was short lived, gaining Royal assent on June 10th 1825 despite having been a very close vote in favour, and £1350000 was allocated from government funds – the rest of the capital required was raised by shares. John Hall, who became secretary of the Company, was acknowledged as a key figure in getting the act finally approved. This included the destruction of the medieval hospital of St Katharine (built in 1148), church (fourteenth century) and graveyards; as well as approximately 1250 houses affecting maybe in excess of 11300 people across 13 acres of land. (See page 24). Parliament also decreed that the rights of the Monarch should be preserved, similarly those of The Master and Brethren. The heirs of people whose monuments were in the church or hospital were allowed to remove them from the custody of the Brethren of the Hospital, and be entitled to the same privileges in other consecrated places. Compensation was to be paid to tenants, but not the actual occupants. Unfortunately, the Master, Taylor, didn't make great representation on the Precinct's behalf, and the Brethren and Sisters at that time were unlikely to have been 'strong fighters'. Nor did Taylor make representation on behalf of the inhabitants, for whom he had direct responsibility. The timing was extraordinary, one of the few gaps in history when a Queen's strong influence was unavailable. It is possible that King George had knowledge of the Chapter's sympathy for the late Queen, so had little or no sympathy with the Precinct. It should also be mentioned that the influence of the City would have been very powerful – historically, the City had never been able to influence this area (re taxes and trade rule, etc); for centuries its efforts were always thwarted by potential Royal authority. Bitter, passionate and strong arguments had been made on both sides of the plan for closure. Actual levels of poverty was one of the most important issues raised. Critics argued that the area was dilapidated if not falling apart, that huge numbers of unemployed 'ruffians' lived there, that opium dens, brothels and other signs of depravity were self evident and sanitary conditions very poor. Certainly there were large numbers of unemployed – inevitable because of the influx of immigrants and the huge numbers of sailors and soldiers made redundant following the end of the Napoleonic War, eight or so years previously – but St Katharine's was comparatively well organised in terms of street cleanliness, rebuilding and modernisation according to the Chapter records, similarly with the constables' handling of law and order. Reports of population differ enormously from 3000 at the lower level to in excess of 11000 at the highest, as though 'spin' was thriving as a vehicle for the enforcement of argument. It was known that many of the known 150 who attended at the Church regularly were decent, good people, working in trade, commerce, manufacturing, as watermen and other work on the river. It was also known that the Church maintained high standards during the services in its devotion, with smart clergy and neatly dressed charity children. The Church was devotedly and affectionately referred to as 'Old Kate'.

'Old Kate'

Sadly, the last service took place on October 29th, 1825 and the sermon was given by the Rev. R.R. Bailey, Chaplain at the Tower. Below is a letter from William Hone, followed by an extract from comments reporting on the final sermon:

To the Editor of the Every-Day Book. Oct. 29, 1825

'Sir,

The ancient and beautiful collegiate church of St. Katharine finally closes tomorrow, previous to its demolition by the St. Katharine's Dock Company. The destruction of an edifice of such antiquity, one of the very few that escaped the great fire of 1666, has excited much public attention. I hope, therefore, that the subject will not be lost sight of in your Every-Day Book. Numbers of the nobility and gentry, who, notwithstanding an earnest appeal was made to them, left the sacred pile to its fate, have lately visited it. In fact, for the beauty and simplicity of its architecture, it has scarcely a rival in London, excepting the Temple church: the interior is ornamented with various specimens of ancient carving; a costly monument of the duke of Exeter, and various others of an interesting kind. This interesting fabric has been sacrificed by the present chapter, consisting of the master, Sir Herbert Taylor, three brethren chaplains, and three sisters, to a new dock company, who have no doubt paid them handsomely for sanctioning the pulling down of the church, the violation of the graves, and the turning of hundreds of poor deserving people out of their homes; their plea is, that they have paid the chapter. I hope, sir, you will pardon the liberty I have taken in troubling you with these particulars; and that you will not forget poor Old Kate, deserted as she is by those whose duty it was to have supported her. I remain,

Your obedient servant,
A NATIVE OF THE PRECINCT.

P. S. There is no more occasion for these docks than for one at the foot of Ludgate-hill.'

'R.R. Bailey, resident chaplain of the Tower, ascended the curious old pulpit of this remarkable structure. This gentleman, whose "History of the Tower" is well known to topographers and antiquaries, appropriately selected for his text, "Go to now, ye that say, to-day or to-morrow we will go into such a city, and continue there a year, and buy and sell and get gain." (James iv. 13.) He discoursed of the frailty of man's purpose, and the insecurity of his institutions, and enjoined hope and reliance on Him whose order ordained and preserves the world in its mutations. He spoke of the "unfeeling and encroaching hand of commerce", which had rudely seized on the venerable fabric, wherein no more shall be said.' (See the Hone Archive in the References.)

Taylor did, however, get a good deal for the removal and costs of moving to Regents Park. The foundation was given an endowment income in excess of £10,000 per annum and the rights of the Monarch was preserved, as were the entitlements of the Master and Brethren, though the links with the old community for which it had been created, were severed. It was rebuilt under the guidance of architect Ambrose Poynter,

St Katharine's Regents Park, now the Danish Church

who was closely associated with John Nash, the designer of Regents Park itself. By his foresight, great care was taken to save and preserve many of the fittings from the original church, including the pulpit, choir stalls and other important monuments and relics.

A magnificent house was built for the Master (much criticised for its luxury and unsuitability for its intended purpose), along with six other houses (three for the Brothers and three for the Sisters), a new chapel (which housed the cherished relics from the old church) and a modest school building. Though small, the school became an important feature locally and remained open until 1915. Gradually, the standard of the Order declined, gaining a poor reputation. In the late 1880s Queen Victoria agreed to the formation of a Jubilee Institute (influenced by Florence Nightingale, among others) to oversee training and supervision of district nurses. It used premises at St Katharine's and the Master became its first president.

Twentieth Century to Present Day

In 1914, under the patronage of Queen Alexandra, the Foundation became the Royal College of St Katharine, moving back to the East End of London, to Bromley Hall in Poplar, and also occupying The Manor House and two other houses. They trained nurses and midwives while also providing for maternity and child health care.

This was followed, in 1919, by the use of the buildings for the West End Hospital For Nervous Diseases. 73 Welbeck Street became the out-patients department while the in-patients moved to the vacated St Katharine's Lodge – the former Master's House of St Katharine's Hospital. Eventually the Foundation moved to Poplar, then on to Limehouse, where it still thrives in a modern form.

CHAPTER TWO

Development of Telford's Docks

————<o>————

Concept

Thomas Telford

The West India Docks opened at Poplar in 1802, designed to receive cargo into warehouse accommodation, and was the first dock in London to solve the problem of loading and unloading with tidal rise and fall. To avoid pilfering, which had previously been a major problem for merchants, the area was surrounded by a high Customs wall. London Docks, opening in 1805, and East India Docks in 1806, soon followed. These new facilities dramatically increased trade to the port; Permission had been given by parliament to allow the owners pricing privileges for a twenty one year period, which effectively gave a monopoly – they could charge high rates to recoup much of their capital investment. Thomas Tooke, an influential businessman and economist who went on to become chairman of the St Katharine Docks Company, saw the opportunity of opening a new dock close to the City, therefore slashing the transport and distribution costs of goods and being able to undercut the expensive rates charged by the other docks further down river. He was well connected with important City figures, and chaired the influential group which included two important members of parliament, banker William Glynn and John Horseley Palmer, who went on to become Governor of the Bank Of England, in developing the idea of a new St Katharine Docks. In choosing the 13 acre site they were well aware that this would be much smaller than other docks, but the central location was felt to be a major advantage and careful design could maximize efficiency within the space available. The pressure on Lord Telford and his colleagues was enormous, as this was an extremely expensive venture, depending for success on good planning, management and profitability.

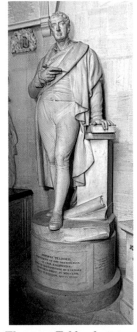

Thomas Telford statue
Courtesy of Westminster Abbey

The Building of St Katharine Docks

St Katharine Docks was built on the East side of The Tower of London, separated only by Little Tower Hill to the West, Upper East Smithfield to the North and Nightingale Lane (now Thomas More Street) Eastwards, separating it from London Docks. Successful bridge and canal engineer Thomas Telford was commissioned as chief engineer, on a salary of £500 per annum, with Thomas Rhodes as resident engineer, on £300 per annum. Telford was particularly concerned to reduce barge and lighters use and pilferage; he achieved this by bringing ships to dock next to the warehouses, to avoid lighters ferrying the cargo from ship to shore, and building high walls around the whole site, providing security. The design was for an entrance lock with an outer gate on the river and swing-bridge above (to allow pedestrian walkway to continue), two inner gates and an entrance basin leading to a west dock and an east dock. Telford's design was brilliant, not least because the Docks were able to function independently of each other via the Central Basin, but it also allowed for the water level to be kept equal between them, while ships could enter at relatively low tides. The warehouses were to have roads directly behind them, which made clever use of the limited land available in such a small area. A fine master's house was designed at the entrance to the outer lock and an impressive office building at the entrance in the northwest corner (opposite the Royal Mint, on the other side of the road) to house directors, management and clerical staff. George Burge won the overall building contract and was commissioned to carry out the plans; this involved clearing the land and excavating the earth before completing all the building work. Beneath was gravel, so the excavated site was lined with a type of concrete, bricked and then grouted to ensure it was watertight. He achieved this by hiring a workforce of 2500; excavation commenced and was completed in 18 months. A massive tonnage of earth was transported to marshy land in Pimlico and Belgravia by river, enabling the landowner, Lord Grosvenor, to build houses in that area. A cast iron swing bridge was built above the Entrance Lock and a second, wrought iron footbridge was built in 1829 between the Central Basin and the East Dock. This was replaced in 1993 and is on view nearby – although built by Thomas Rhodes, it became known as the Telford Bridge. Early estimates allowed for in excess of 120 ships, as well as barges and various other support craft. The water in the lock was kept filled by using two steam engines, provided by James Watts, which were housed in an engine house beside the lock. It could be filled in five and a half minutes, a great feat at that time. Ships had a clearance of at least 20ft from two hours before to half an hour after neap tides, and longer at spring tides. Unloading time was improved by an incredible 4/5ths – early lifting power was manual, with treadmill type pulley systems (more detail is given under 'casual workers') which were later replaced by steam and then hydraulic cranes (some may still be seen on the walls of International House and featured at the entrance to the lock). Telford had been very concerned about safety issues during this period; the intense pressure on the workforce to use all speed made much of the work more dangerous. In October 1827 there was an exceptionally high tide, so the bank was breached and the area was flooded within fifteen minutes; amazingly, there was no loss of life, though it took a fortnight to pump the excavations dry, putting the scheme further behind schedule. With the opening of the West Dock in 1828, work was then concentrated on the East Dock, completed in 1829. On the river front, adjacent to the Tower of London, Irongate Wharf had been in existence since the 16th century, used for unloading mainly grain; the new, 170' long St Katharine's Steam Packet Wharf was built alongside, west of the Dock gates, to accommodate ships that were too big to get into the Docks. This contract was given to Thomas Carpe, selected because his was the cheapest tender. He began work in February 1829, but disregarded the contract specification and some of Rhodes' instructions; he dug away too much gravel below the foundations of the previous wharf and the wall collapsed, fortunately without loss of life – Carpe was dismissed and the damage repaired. Much of the Docks' original equipment remained in use until the eventual closure.

The Warehouses

Architect Sir Phillip Hardwick designed the six storey warehouses in yellow-grey London stock bricks, with windows made of cast iron. Surrounding the Docks, they were built right to the edge of the water, with some bays recessed to accommodate cranes that could load or unload straight into or from the warehouses, or, on the landward side, into carts and later lorries; this avoided double handling. These buildings were 470 feet long and 140 feet deep (143 x 43 metres) and had extensive underground vaults. The ground floors were left half open to allow for transport and working areas, supported by massive cast-iron Tuscan colonnades. The vast interiors were divided into smaller areas by fire walls

Opening of St Katharine Docks
Courtesy of Greenwich Maritime Museum

with 6 mm thick iron doors, which also allowed goods to be kept separate for customs purposes. By the 1830s, the warehouses were storing more than 50000 tons of merchandise. In 1860, the T shaped warehouse was completed, designed by George Aitchison – it became known as Ivory House and is the only one to still survive, though in a very different form.

The official opening was on 25th October 1828, the East Dock opening one year later. There was an invited audience of 10000 people, including George Carr Glynn, the banker who worked hard to support the new capital venture. The first ship to enter the Docks was the Elizabeth, with a band playing on board and flying the flags of every nation, symbolically bringing the world to St Katharine Docks. The second ship to enter was a Russian trader, the Mary, which was 343 tons. She had an assortment of Russian cargo and put ashore forty war

Thomas Tooke 1774 – 1858

veteran pensioners from Greenwich Hospital, all of whom had served under Admiral Lord Nelson at the Battle of Trafalgar in 1805. It is interesting to note that there was no dignitary to officiate at the opening ceremony; suggestions were made that this may have been due to the controversy over the ancient hospital closure, or that doubts remained whether the Docks were necessary or capable of making good profit.

Chairman

The first chairman was Thomas Tooke, of Russian descent, a well-known economist and established business leader in the City who had played a very important part in lobbying for the creation of the Docks. He was also considered a great expert in nineteenth century monetary thought. William Glynn and John Horsley were fellow directors, as were two prominent members of Parliament and various other powerful, successful businessmen.

CHAPTER THREE

The Working Docks

————◁○▷————

Initially, business was very good, with cheap tariffs and easy road access to the markets ensuring early success, but rail access dramatically improved for the other docks and the narrow entrance locks meant no access for the newer steamships, which were getting bigger – even at the opening ships were sailing by which were too big for St Katharine's. In the 1830s the Dock Company bought further, highly secure warehousing in Cutler Street (near Aldgate), sold to them by the East India Company. By 1864 it had become necessary for St Katharine's and near neighbour London Docks to merge and they then took over the newer Victoria Dock. Gradually, government eased restrictions on trade of imported and exported goods, which led to less storage time needed in the warehouses, as did quicker disbursement by improved road and rail networks, so lowering the profit and dividends to shareholders. Irongate Wharf, owned by the General Steam

Ships in the Docks

Navigation Company, was destroyed by fire in 1846, but rebuilt and trading eight years later. Trade involving these wharves was mainly with Europe, particularly wines and spirits, with general cargo and fruit in the summer months. The famous daytrip paddle steamers Crested Eagle and Royal Sovereign used these wharves, among others. In 1909, the Port of London Authority took over the management of the Docks, as it did with most of the others. By the 1930s the General Steam Navigation Company had started to pioneer using containers for shipping cargo. St Katharine Docks eventually closed in 1968.

The Workers

Though the permanent staff varied, early on there were 35 officers, with approximately 200+ staff and 250 regular labourers; this was supplemented as required by a casual workforce of 1700. A class structure quickly developed, in which rank, class and division became very important. Wage levels mattered, but so did the type of work, as well as respectability. Workers who unloaded guano (see page 48) were well paid, but considered very far down the dock hierarchy. Casuals who unpacked the crates of ivory and were subject to venomous bites from trapped insects were also looked down upon.

Clerical / Bookkeeping

This aspect was very complex. Each commodity had its own set of procedures and diversity in the way it needed to be handled – this all then had to be costed, recorded and billed. To give an example taken from an original document at the Docklands Museum: 'Tea required a landing and housing rate, comprising landing, wharfage, housing, separating, weighing, furnishing landing weights, examining and turning out and in for damage, mending, laying down for private inspection, lotting, nailing down, placing in delivery pile and delivery by

								16 lbs.
TEA.	s. d.	s. d.	s. d.	s. d.	s. d.	s. d.	s. d.	s. d.
Landing and Housing Rate, comprising landing, wharfage, housing, separating into chops, weighing, furnishing landing weights, examining and turning out and in for damage, mending, laying down for private inspection, lotting, nailing down, placing in delivery pile, and delivery by land..............	3 6	2 7	2 1	1 9½	1 7	1 3	0 9½	0 5
Management Rate, comprising the same operations as the landing and housing rate, also laying down for public sale, attendance whilst on show, extra warehouse-room, and any other operations consequent thereon, and delivery by land	4 4	3 3	2 7	2 1	1 9½	1 4	0 10½	0 6
Additional, if shipped	0 5	0 4	0 3	0 2	0 1½	0 1½	0 1	0 0½
Rent, per week	0 1	0 0¾	0 0½	0 0½	0 0½	0 1½	0 1	0 0½

Journal entries
Courtesy of Docklands Museum

land. Then a Management rate was added, comprising the same operations as the landing and housing rate, also laying down for public sale, attendance whilst on show, extra warehouse room, and any other operations consequent thereon, and delivery by land'.

Stevedores

Stevedores were among the most skilled dock workers, and so enjoyed status at the top of the scale. In loading the ships they were able to maximise the space aboard, while ensuring they were 'packed' in the correct order, for unloading at different ports; they also needed to know how to balance the cargo in the holds to avoid the danger of capsizing. This work was often undertaken in dangerous and difficult conditions, so was highly paid. A gang of stevedores would be led by a master stevedore, ensuring work was done as quickly as possible.

Lightermen

These men came next in order of seniority. They were highly skilled at manoeuvring up, down and across the Thames by using the currents and tides. Apprenticed for between five and seven years, they were tightly controlled by rules laid down by the Company of Watermen and Lightermen, and by acts of parliament. The boats they used became popular early in the 1800s, because the Thames was seriously overloaded with ships which needed to transfer their cargo to the riverside wharves, prior to the advent of the enclosed docks. The early standard design changed little over the years, except in size and material – wood becoming iron and eventually steel. A minimum of two men was needed to steer the vessels around the river by the use of sweeps, which were long oars, with the lightermen using their knowledge of the tides and currents to carry them to the place required. As steam power developed, small, powerful tugs were built to tow up to a maximum of six of these lighters. In the 1950s, 8000 lighters were in use, with more than 250 tugs.

Skilled Workers

Below these levels was a whole array of skilled workers, including coopers, porters, riggers, markers, samplers, tallymen, warehousemen, sail makers, pilers, baulkers, blenders and many more.

Dockers

Next came the ordinary dockers, who were the general workers. These employees considered themselves very superior to the casuals, described on the next page.

Dockers unloading from a crane

Working in the hold

Casuals

These were a pool of unskilled hopefuls at the bottom of the hierarchy. The group also had its own pecking order; truckers, who moved cargo from the quayside to the warehouse or transit-shed, were the least skilled of all. Strength varied amongst these men – one job, for men with strong leg muscles, was to work a form of treadmill crane (similar to the hamster playwheel principle); between six and eight men would work inside a large drum, lifting or lowering loads on a pulley rope system by using a walking motion while stationary. Another group was chosen because of arm strength, the men working winches by pulling on ropes; this included dragging ships in and out of the Docks, while another group pulled and pushed the various types of truck – they were said to cover more than thirty miles per day and average more than six miles per hour. These men stood near the dock entrance, hoping to be taken on for a day, half day or even an hour, as and when required by the foremen. This method was referred to as 'The Call On' and was extremely harsh, the foreman often selecting family and friends first, with bribery also being an inducement. On the other hand, if a ship was unloaded quicker than scheduled, a bonus called 'the share' was given to the foreman, to distribute how he wanted – it was in the foreman's interest, therefore, to take on the most reliable workers, judging them for strength and toughness. These people depended on the amount of work that could be done – a change of wind might allow another ship to enter the dock, while the east wind was dreaded as it stopped ships from moving in – they therefore lived on the edge of serious poverty.

The Unions

The forerunners to trade unions were the Livery Guilds, who were very powerful in their time. Indeed, the Lightermen and Watermen's Guild, who had pressed for the 'Free Water Clause' in 1799, saw that it was never repealed – this became a major factor in the reduced profits from dock investment. Some observers are curious that 'the guilds' are regarded by many in much higher esteem than the trade unions, historically; these people were all struggling to achieve fairness in the work place, against injustice often shown by employers, as exposed by writers such as Charles Dickens.

Demonstrations in Copenhagen Fields to protest at the deportation of the Tolpuddle Martyrs, 21 April 1834

Courtesy of the Tolpuddle Martyrs Museum

Call-on Bell, Ivory House

Following violent protests by the Luddites in 1811/12, Parliament repealed the Combination Acts of 1799–1800. Trade unions were now becoming a political force and developing an important voice. In 1834 the Whig government encouraged the police to arrest six agricultural workers in Tolpuddle, a village in Dorset, who had formed a trade union. They were found guilty (of at least 'dubious' charges) and transported to a penal colony in Australia; they became known as the Tolpuddle Martyrs. This triggered protests throughout the country, but was ignored by the authorities. Short term, this discouraged trade union membership, weakening some unions and breaking many; after much further pressure they were reprieved and returned to the UK. By the 1850s, with the improvement in the economy, the movement had grown by leaps and bounds, with membership growth from 100,000 in the early 1850s to nearly a million by 1874. In 1872 there was a dockers strike; they did achieve some success, but dock owners were successful in countering this by using more stringent methods for paying casual staff. Accommodation in East London tended to be extremely poor; the 1890 Housing Act made local councils responsible for providing tenants with decent accommodation, but this didn't really help until well into the next century, so poverty, hunger and slum living was the norm. Then, in 1888, a deservedly successful strike by ladies at the Bryant and May factory in Bow, the 'Matchgirls Strike', ignited hope which encouraged other trade unionists to fight for better conditions and pay. In 1889 there was a second important success for gas workers on strike at Beckton, East London. What became known as the Great Dock Strike also took place in 1889, sparked by an incident at the West India Docks, where a cargo ship, the Lady Armstrong, was being unloaded. The dock manager stopped the bonus that had been earned by the men for fast unloading (called the 'plus rates'), so the workers downed tools and went on strike. These workers were casuals, whose wretched employment rules using the 'call on' system and appalling living conditions have already been set out above. A relatively

Ben Tillett (1860–1943)
Courtesy of Bristol Library

successful union had been set up by Ben Tillett, generally regarded as the skilful organiser behind the strike, known as The Tea Operatives and General Labourers Association, which was one of the few to offer membership to casual workers – Tillett rushed to the West India Docks and telegraphed his friend and important trade unionist, Tom Mann, who quickly joined him there. Tillett well understood that the real power against the docks management lay with the Amalgamated Stevedores union, lead by Tom McCarthy, the aristocrats of the dockside; to his great personal credit he achieved their backing, so gaining not only their 'management clout', but also their funds.

Within two days, on the 14th August, the Great Dock Strike had begun. All dock labour was withdrawn and other unions gave their support, including the Engineering Union; their leader was John Burns, who had gained great public support following his speaking out against poverty in London over the previous several years. Some estimates put striker numbers at about 130000 at its peak. Regular protest parades were arranged to the City of London; respect was gained because of the peaceful nature and large numbers marching in these parades. The Times, which was said by some to be supportive, reported around 100000 present when they rallied in Hyde

Butler's Wharf

Park. Henry Lafone, manager of Butler's Wharf (opposite St Katharine's across the Thames), was a great help as he paid his own 300 workers one shilling per day while they were on strike, and negotiated hard with the strike committee to help break the deadlock.

By mid September the dock companies had agreed a pay increase that was substantial enough for the workers to honourably claim victory, and the strike to end. It had lasted five agonizing weeks and gained a reputation for its good organisation, not short on near military discipline of pickets and others, with respect for law and order. During that period, clothes and furniture was pawned, collections were made from the public, the Salvation Army provided 10000 loaves of bread daily, churches created soup kitchens and shops did all they could, but starvation came very close. Ultimate help came from Australian workers, who sent a massive £30000, enough to fund the strikers to a successful end on September 16th, 1889. This summary is short and not meant to imply that mistakes had not been made, or that some motives may have been questionable. Nevertheless, respect should be considered for the example set by good, working class people who were struggling against squalor and starvation. They didn't revolt, as in some other countries, but showed control and hope that they would become better valued and respected, in a very dignified manner. Incidentally, these years influenced the fledgling Labour Party, and the people concerned were the predecessors of those involved in the nearby Cable Street protest and, of course, the Blitz.

Thames Barges

These majestic sailing boats were an essential part of commerce on the Thames during the nineteenth century. Having a flat-bottomed hull, they could navigate in as little as one metre of water and remained flat instead of keeling to one side when aground on mud flats or sand banks, making them ideal for navigating in the shallow waters of the creeks, inlets and tributaries in the Thames and its estuary. They could lower the masts for passing under bridges and were also highly economical because of their ability to use the tides to travel up and down the river (the Thames has two low and two

Thames Barges near Butler's Wharf in the 1880s

high tides each day). They were also used extensively for coastal work and across to Ireland and the Continent. Furthermore, Thames barges were able to sail empty, without ballast, saving time and money. At their peak there were more than 2000 trading on the river. Prior to their arrival, horses and carts had been the main carriers, obviously needing one man, a horse and a cart, carrying a maximum of one ton; along came the Thames barges, able to carry up to 200 tons, with no fuel costs and greatly increased speed, putting thousands of cart carriers (and their horses) out of business. Typically, they would load farm products, bricks, building materials, and many other items, bringing them to the customers and to within range of the main markets. The distinctive rusty red sails were made of flax, and the colour was caused by the waterproofing treatment, originally made up of cod oil, red ochre and seawater. Eventually, engines were added for greater efficiency. There are further details about Thames Barges, particularly the Lady Daphne, later in the book.

Dockmaster's House, St Katharine Docks

CHAPTER FOUR

Cargo

———◦———

The Docks developed a worldwide reputation for handling valuable, largely luxury cargo. The list is extensive and included carpets, china, coal, dried fruits, hops, indigo (important dye), ivory (both elephant and walrus), marble, matches, mohair, silk, exotic bird feathers, perfume, shells, spices, tallow (for candles), tea, tortoiseshell, turtles, wine, spirits and wool. Right up until the 1930s there was a dynamic, thriving trade in these luxury items and the Docks were referred to as the world's focal point for the greatest concentration of portable wealth.

Wool

More than 30 acres of warehousing was allocated to the storage of wool, holding more than half a million bales. This was one of the most important cargoes, both for the nation and St Katharine's, as historically, wool could only be exported through designated ports, including London. In the fourteenth century raw wool was specifically disallowed for export for a period, so weavers from other countries (particularly the Flemish) came over to make cloth and a new industry was created. The ban only lasted for seven years, but the textile trade grew and flourished. By the nineteenth century import of wool had become huge, mainly from the colonies of Australia and New Zealand, though also from the Falkland Isles, South Africa, China, South America and the Middle East. This included, of course, the importing of exotic and luxury cashmere, camel and goat hair. Wool sales took place on site every six weeks, each lasting two weeks, with auctions every day at 3 pm and bidding by brokers. The handling involved was on such a scale that 1200 people were required at times. In the House of Lords, the Woolsack, famously the seat of the Lord Chancellor, was introduced by King Edward III back in the fourteenth century as a symbol of wealth, acknowledging the importance of wool trade for the country.

Tea

Dutch traders were the first to import tea to Europe in 1610. This was very successful, and so teapots also became an important import from China. Drinking tea was first fashionable in Holland, then England – following the Great Plague of 1665 and the Great Fire of 1666, pleasure gardens became popular in London, where the drinking of tea was taken, often in the fresh air. Partly due to its ease of production and because the necessity to boil the water made it safer, tea became more popular than coffee. By the 1750s China tea and tea services were a necessary part of most upper and middle class homes, while tax was imposed on tea in 1689 and not removed until 1964, which led to extensive smuggling. Thanks to the indus-

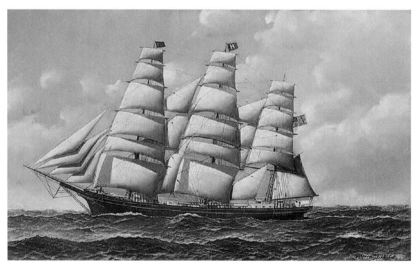

Tea Clipper

46

trial revolution large numbers of workers needed nourishment; tea served the purpose well, mixed with sugar (another big import) and milk. By the 1800s tea had become so popular in the UK that it created an imbalance of trade with China; the East India Company paid for the tea with opium grown in India, taken to China in the famous Clipper sailing ships. This trade was brought to an end by Britain's Opium Wars with China between 1839 and 1842 and the East India Company developed tea growing in North East India to compensate, while the opium clippers were adapted for tea transport and sales boomed. The China trade resumed and speed was obviously of prime importance; the legendary annual clipper races took place, the most famous in 1866, when no less than three of the first ships arrived on the same tide. The race lasted three months and the winner was the Taepin; the second ship arrived twenty minutes later and the three captains (incidentally, all Scottish) and crews shared the prize money. Indian teas gradually became more popular than Chinese (and Japanese). Tea came on stream from Ceylon (now Sri Lanka) in 1867 and Africa towards the end of the nineteenth century. Up to 32000 tons was handled each year, and was sorted and packaged on site. Tea sales recovered after the Second World War, but by the 1950s instant coffee also became popular; tea remains the leader, though often in teabag form.

Tallow

This important past import to St Katharine's played a key role in everyday needs. Made from animal fat, prior to the 1800s it was used for city, town, commercial and domestic lighting. By the time St Katharine Docks opened cheaper candle components had replaced tallow, but it remained in great demand for cooking, soap making and numerous other uses. In 1842 a dock worker at St Katharine's was convicted at The Old Bailey for stealing twenty pounds of tallow (value eight shillings) and imprisoned for twelve months. In 1853 Prime Minister Palmerston removed duty on tallow, 'to improve public cleanliness'.

Guano

Used as a fertilizer, this smelly commodity was the excrement of mainly seabirds, bats and seals. It was imported from various ocean islands and South America, becoming one of the main exports from Peru, the biggest exporter in the nineteenth century. William Gibbs became the most important trader in this commodity – by the 1850s, guano, rich in nitrogen and phosphates, exceeded 200000 tons imported to the UK each year. Mr Gibbs became the richest 'commoner in the country' and a Music Hall ditty about him became famous: 'William Gibbs made his dibs, Selling the turds of foreign birds'. Eventually, cheaper products replaced guano, so by the 1880s sales had dropped dramatically.

Tortoiseshell

The name is a misnomer, since the majority of tortoiseshell came from turtles, though also from larger tortoises. The main contributor was the hawksbill turtle, from the South Asia

'To the sea', one of the collection of sculptures around the Docks by Paula Haughney, sculptor

Seas and the Caribbean, down to the coast of Brazil. It is now an endangered species, and though its history is fascinating, the method of extraction was often extremely cruel and has thankfully been forbidden since the 1970s. Tortoiseshell was used extensively in the luxury market for items such as intricately decorated jewellery and valuable tea caddies, as well as more common items such as combs and knitting needles. Though expensive, it has been very popular because of its beautiful mottled appearance, strength and durability, and is comfortably warm against the skin. Turtle shell is classified as a natural thermoplastic, so is softened by the application of heat and can be moulded into various shapes, which are retained upon cooling; very versatile for manufacture.

Mother of Pearl

Also known as Nacre, from the Arabic word naqqarah, meaning shell, this was another very important item imported to St Katharine's from as far away as the seas in Asia. It is made up of mainly calcium carbonate, formed by millions of crystal platelets and looks very beautiful, hence why it was used for jewellery and adorning trinkets and small containers, as well as soaps, face creams and other beauty preparations, floor tiles and high quality industrial instruments.

Exotic Feathers

These came from a huge range of exotic birds, including ostrich, osprey, egret, ibis, heron, pelican, bustard, peacock and bird of Paradise, to provide the millinery trade for use in decorating hats for the ladies fashion market. The height of the 'plume boom' was in the late 1880s and was a big earner for the docks trade. These feathers came from all over the world, supplied by plume hunters who tended to shoot the adult bird, often leaving its young to starve; this eventually led to a shortage and near extinction of some species. By the 1890s the RSPB (Royal Society For The Protection of Birds)

'Exotic Birds', sculpture by Paula Haughney

became effective in pressurising for reform. The rarity of osprey feathers became a great issue and Queen Alexandra banned the use of them at Court, while similar pressure groups worked hard in America to reduce the 'plume boom' emotively referred to as 'murderous millinery'. Eventually, the Plumage Act of 1921 prohibited the sale, hire or exchange of the plumage and skins of certain wild birds, putting a virtual end to this trade.

Scent

Perfumes from Grasse and elsewhere were imported. Musk bags of the musk-ox, civet (from the animal of the same name), ambergris from whales and other foul smelling ingredients were all collected here for the scent industry. The firms using the factory at St Katharine's avoided duty on alcohol added, as it was for export only and therefore not liable.

Indigo

Compressed blocks of the deep blue powder were imported in huge quantities from India and other colonies, useful as the most colour fast dye for fabrics, not least denim. Part of one of the warehouses was called Indigo House. Workers handling the substance were easily identifiable, as their hands and clothes became the same colour as the dye.

Marble

The Marble Quay handled fine quality material that came from Italy in particular.

Used for carving and decoration, ivory was a major luxury product. As mentioned, the only warehouse still standing came to be known as Ivory House – this was due to the vast quantities of ivory that passed through it. At its peak in the 1870s it was reckoned that nearly 200 tons of ivory covered its floors annually, amounting to almost 4000 dead elephants. There were also imports of hippopotamus and walrus tusks. Aside from ivory, the warehouse handled other luxury imports such as perfume, shells and wine in the expansive basement vaults. Until the late nineteenth century, London was the principal importer of ivory.

Five hundred tons were imported into the capital every year, mainly from the East and West coasts of Africa. Smaller tusks were sent on to India to make bangles, toys and board games, while the larger, softer tusks were shipped to famous

Ivory

carving centres in Germany and France where they were carved into ornate pieces such as crucifixes, paper cutters and delicate napkin rings. London itself used the ivory mainly to produce piano keys and billiard balls, while there was a thriving industry in Sheffield making elegant cutlery handles. Most of these were luxury items made for the elite of Victorian England and the rest of Europe as symbols of affluence.

Ivory House

CHAPTER FIVE

Ship Chandlery

————◄◦►————

The following notes were put together by staff at Nauti-calia, who have a fine shop in today's St Katharine's; they sell replicas of items that were used in the old days, some of which are still in use by boat owners today.

Boatswain's Call

A boatswain's call, pipe or bosun's whistle is a pipe or non-diaphragm type whistle used on naval ships by a boatswain. Historically, this was used to pass commands to the crew when the voice could not be heard over the sounds of the sea. Because of its high pitch, it was audible over the bad weather and activities of the crew.

Boatswain's Call

Pewter Hip Flask

Hip flasks were traditionally made of pewter, silver or even glass. The hip flask began to appear in the form recognized today in the eighteenth century, initially used by members of the gentry. Women boarding docked ships would smuggle in gin via makeshift flasks created from pigs' bladders, hidden within their petticoats.

The 'Kings Shilling' Tankard

Legend tells us that eighteenth century Royal Navy press gangs (recruitment officers) used to hide a signing-up bounty, the 'King's Shilling', in the 'free pints' that they offered to unsuspecting sailors in waterside taverns. Drinking the beer was deemed to be acceptance of the money and commitment to recruitment in the King's service, full of harsh discipline and dreadful food! The glass-bottomed tankard was therefore said to have been invented so that men would spot the trick before it was too late.

Gimballed Oil Lamp

This lamp was used to illuminate ship's cabins at the end of the nineteenth century. The lamp has had many names in Denmark: "The 90 years lamp", "Esso lamp" and "Saloon

Gimballed oil lamp

lamp". A gimballed lamp mount consists of two rings mounted on axes at right angles to each other, so that the oil lamp itself will remain suspended in a horizontal plane between them regardless of any motion of its support.

Tide Clock

A tide clock is specially designed to keep track of the Moon's apparent motion around the Earth. Along many coastlines the Moon contributes the major part (67 percent) of the combined lunar and solar tides. Owing to the Moon's orbital progress, it takes a particular point on the Earth on average 24 hours 50.5 minutes to rotate under the Moon, so the time between high lunar tides fluctuates between 12 and 13 hours. A tide clock is divided into two six hour long tidal periods that shows the average length of time between high and low tide in a semi-diurnal tide region, such as most areas of the Atlantic Ocean. Therefore, compared with the actual time between the high lunar tides, tide clocks gain approximately 15 minutes per month and must be reset periodically. Tides have an inherent lead or lag known as the lunitidal interval that is different at every location, and so tidal clocks are set for the time when the local lunar high tide occurs.

Stormglass

The Stormglass was, in so far as we know, first used in about 1750 by sailing ships to predict stormy weather. The first proper report concerning its use on a ship was by Robert Fitzroy aboard HMS Beagle during the Darwin Expeditions of 1831–1836. A Stormglass is a simple weather forecasting instrument. Crystals form in the liquid and change their appearance in reaction to various meteorological influences. Captain Fitzroy developed his own specific liquid, and during his voyage documented the changes in the crystals along with the changes in the weather, concluding that simple forecasts could be made.

Stormglass

Classic Survey Compass

D.W. Brunton was a mining engineer in Colorado, USA, when he took out the patent for his versatile new dry compass in 1894. Within four years he was able to claim it was "in use in every country from Australia to Alaska". Ideal for surveying unexplored terrains, surveyors mapped out new lands and territories and chartered coastlines, carrying their compact, solid brass Brunton's compasses in leather cases slung over their shoulders. It was used as a plumb, hand level, clinometer, sighting compass, prismatic compass, and for obtaining horizontal and vertical angles, for preliminary surface surveying, topography, geological field work and reconnaissance.

Quarter-size Vernier Sextant

Full-size vernier sextants were, in skilled hands, instruments of great accuracy, practicality and beauty – a joy to own and use, but also essential to the safety of the ship. Royal Navy Captain John Campbell developed the instrument in 1757. Crucially, his invention appeared at about the same time as the first accurate portable chronometers, and the combination of the two transformed navigation from guesswork to science, saving countless lives at sea. A sextant is an instrument used to measure the angle between any two visible objects. Its primary use is to determine the angle between a celestial object and the horizon, which is known as the object's altitude. Making this measurement is known as sighting the object, shooting the object, or taking a sight, and is an essential part of celestial navigation. The angle and the time when it was measured can be used to calculate a position line on a nautical or aeronautical chart. Common uses of the sextant include sighting the sun at solar noon and sighting Polaris at night, to find one's latitude (in northern latitudes). Sighting the height of a landmark can give a measure of distance off and, held horizontally, a sextant can measure angles between objects for a position on a chart. A sextant can also be used to measure the lunar distance between the Moon and another celestial object (e.g., star, planet) in order to determine Greenwich time, which is important as it can then be used to determine the longitude. The scale of a sextant has a length of 1/6 of a turn (60°); hence the sextant's name (sextāns, -antis is the Latin word for "one sixth").

Inclinometer

An inclinometer or clinometer is an instrument used on board for measuring the list of a ship in still water and the roll in rough water.

Brass Ship's Bell

A ship's bell is used to indicate the time aboard and hence regulate the sailors' duty watches. The bell itself is usually made of brass or bronze and has the ship's name engraved or cast on it. The ship's cook (or his staff) traditionally has the job of shining the ship's bell. Unlike civil clock bells, the

Brass Ship's Bell

strikes do not accord to the number of the hour, instead there are eight bells, one for each half-hour of a four-hour watch. In the age of sailing watches were timed with a 30-minute hourglass – bells would be struck every time the glass was turned, and in a pattern of pairs for easier counting, with any odd bells at the end of the sequence. At midnight on New Year's Eve sixteen bells would be struck – eight bells for the old year and eight bells for the new.

Portable Brass Sundial

Inspired by originals in the Science Museum, the gnomon, which casts the shadow, can be set for latitude on a sliding scale, and the whole instrument oriented in the meridian by means of a magnetic compass in the base. A spirit level and height-adjustable legs ensure that the instrument is used upright.

Aneroid Barometer

Invented in 1843 by French scientist Lucien Vidi, it uses a small, flexible metal box called an aneroid cell (capsule), which is made from an alloy of beryllium and copper. The evacuated capsule (or usually more capsules) is prevented from collapsing by a strong spring. Small changes in external air pressure cause the cell to expand or contract. This expansion and contraction drives mechanical levers such that

Aneroid Barometer

the tiny movements of the capsule are amplified and displayed on the face of the aneroid barometer. The mechanism is made deliberately "stiff" so that tapping the barometer reveals whether the pressure is rising or falling as the pointer moves. Using barometric pressure and the pressure tendency (the change of pressure over time) has been used in weather forecasting since the late nineteenth century. When used in combination with wind observations, reasonably accurate short-term forecasts can be made.

Cabin Clock

The first chronometers that could accurately keep time on board a ship were developed in the 1700s. The time on a chronometer would have been set at that of the Greenwich Observatory in London – knowing the time of a fixed location allowed the ship's navigator to know the difference between the ship's position and the Greenwich Meridian, thus determining the ship's longitude.

Naval Officers and Pocket Telescopes

A classic four drawer, 12 times magnification telescope is typical of those used by eighteenth century naval officers. The Admiralty, having experimented with higher magnifications, had decided that this was about the optimum for use at sea, so concentrated instead on developing practical features such as the slide-out hood for reducing glare when the sun was high. It is made from solid brass tubing bound with stitched leather, protected in a brass-buckled leather case, and would have been a highly prized possession. It has a 35mm object lens and its length fully extended is 18" (closed 7"). Brass is used in boat and ship fittings, propellers and submerged bearings because of its resistance to salt water corrosion.

Gimballed Ships Compass

The face of the compass generally highlights the cardinal points of north, south, east and west. Often, compasses are built as a standalone sealed instrument with a magnetized bar or needle turning freely upon a pivot, or moving in a fluid, thus able to point in a northerly and southerly direction. The compass greatly improved the safety and efficiency of travel, especially ocean travel. It can be used to calculate heading, with a sextant to calculate latitude, and with a marine chronometer to calculate longitude, thus providing a much improved navigational capability that has only been recently supplanted by modern devices such as the Global Positioning System (GPS).

CHAPTER SIX

Later Life of The Docks

The War Years

The area of the Docks was severely damaged in the Blitz of the Second World War (1939–45). On the 7th September 1940, St Katharine's was badly bombed; most of the warehouses in the East Basin were damaged and were subsequently demolished; the fire that raged was fuelled by big stocks of timber, sugar, tar, rum and a great tonnage of other highly inflammable material – some reports stated that smoke went two miles up into the sky and that the whole of St Katharine Docks was engulfed in flame. There was various other damage and the company office buildings in the North West corner were destroyed. The neighbouring Tower Of London suffered several direct hits, luckily affecting eighteenth and nineteenth century buildings rather than the older ones. Nearby Trinity House was very badly damaged, though Samuel Wyatt's superb facade was left intact. St George in the

London Blitz 1940
Photo U.S. Information Agency

*Fire crews battle to save St Katharine's at the height
of the Blitz, 1940*
East London Advertiser

East was gutted, but thankfully the classic Hawksmoor exterior survived. Most of the riverside buildings that were destroyed along the river and in nearby Wapping have been rebuilt, thankfully respecting the style of the old buildings in most cases.

Decline of The Docks

A constant loss of revenue for the owners was caused by the 'Free Water Clause', which was part of a law passed in 1799, allowing lightermen the right to enter docks without charge, intended to give them the same freedom in docks as they enjoyed on the open river. In practice, it enabled them to either collect or deliver goods to and from ships for storage elsewhere, or to load, ready for export, avoiding the quay dues or warehouse cost. This deeply affected the profits of docks such as St Katharine's and increased the profits of its competitors. Despite vigorous lobbying, future legislation continued to allow this. As Telford's vision was for the handling of sailing ships, some critics argued that the entry point could have been deeper and wider – it was certainly true that even on opening day steamships were passing by that were already too big for the facility. Steamships continued to increase in size and newer docks downstream offered cheaper berthing. St Katharine's gradually lost its unique position advantage next to the City as the road and rail network developed along the Thames. Coasters up to 1000 tons became the biggest that the Docks could handle. From 1909, the Port of London Authority took over the running of St Katharine Docks, similar to most of the others; despite this, because of having too many different authorities and dock companies, agreement could not be reached as to how to deepen the main channel and make the other improvements necessary to allow bigger ships to move more easily upstream. Container vessels changed the entire seascape; by the 1960s there were great opportunities for the new, vast Tilbury Docks, despite it having had very serious difficulties in the early days, when it lowered its tariffs to attract new business, thus further hurting upsteam docks forced to do the same in order to compete. London lost trade to other ports, which had faster handling times and cheaper warehouse facilities and distribution costs. Continental ports such as Antwerp, Hamburg and Rotterdam expanded rapidly and efficiently. Despite its small size, St Katharine's survived for some time by adapting as a storage depot, with lighters ferrying cargo from elsewhere and utilizing its 116000 square metres of storage space, but eventually, in 1968, the Docks were finally closed and sold to the Greater London Council.

The Derelict Years

Damaged buildings were left largely abandoned and derelict following the carnage of the war years, with others becoming disused as the area declined. Most of the East Basin remained as open ground, neglected and deserted. Following closure, numerous artists set up studios in the warehouses, and there are many happy memories from people who recall playing in the area as children. Some of the bombing scenes in the 1969 film 'Battle of Britain' were filmed in the Docks, and in 1973 a fire seriously damaged 'B' Warehouse, the one remaining of the six original Telford and Hardwicke warehouses.

Rising from the Ashes: St Katharine's Haven and Marina

Following its closure, The Port of London Authority sold St Katharine Docks to the Greater London Council. A competition was then held, in 1969, inviting the best design to regenerate the semi derelict warehouses and quays – Taylor Woodrow won and was awarded a 125 year lease for the Docks in 1969. Peter Drew, an engineer and architect, joined Taylor Woodrow, and became a protégé of chairman Frank (later Lord) Taylor. A new company was formed, St Katharine by the Tower Ltd, headed by Drew, who was the driving force behind what became the 'Haven' and is now the Marina. He moved into the historical Dockmaster's House, originally designed and lived in by Telford, and dominated the area for the next twenty years while renovating the Docks. It is said that Desmond Plummer, the Tory GLC leader, was insistent that a boat haven should be included; Drew was originally opposed to this, but gradually became captivated by the grandeur of the old Thames Barges and, most likely, the other links with the past and its history. Numerous aspects were considered, then changed or rejected, with work commencing in September 1970. The project engineer was Ove Arup and Partners, working with architects Renton, Howard, Wood, Levin Associates (now RHWL who still have an office in Ivory House). Part of the estate was sold to J. Lyons and Co., who then built the Tower Hotel on the site, contributing substantially to the initial capital cost of the whole venture. Planning involved Offices, shops and restaurants, renovation of Ivory

House into luxury letting apartments, development of social housing, which became known as South Quay (in East Dock), and further upmarket flats (also in East Dock). At one point an Underground Station was intended, on the proposed Fleet Line, and would have been between Fenchurch Street and Wapping; although an extension was eventually built eastwards on the Jubilee Line, it went by a different route, south of the Thames.

The development has often been cited as a model example of successful urban regeneration and a catalyst to further development in London Docks, then eastwards to Canary Wharf.

The Current Owners

Soon after they bought St Katharine's, the owner of Max Holdings and his colleagues arranged an open meeting at the Tower Hotel to present their intentions for the improvements they wanted to undertake in order to improve standards and viability. They clearly stated that their intention was as an investment, with the eventual aim of selling to realise profit. It was also apparent that despite their business priority, there was an understanding re their responsibility towards high standards in general and the historical aspects of the area. Their clear, straightforward and professional approach was appreciated. It is understood that International House is now producing a better return in rents because of business efficiency and that Commodity Quay is well on track with its redevelopment. We have also seen many smaller but significant improvements; ladies are no longer in danger with their high heels on the footbridge close to the Dickens Inn, and the spiral staircase on the other side is no longer an accident hazard. It is now a great pleasure to walk along the new pontoon in West Dock, stretching the whole length of International House. I gather that boat occupancy is very good and that all the new investment in equipment is to a very high standard. We now have many more seats around, and approximately thirty new lamp posts are being installed (like those already here, provided by Taylor Woodrow, similar to those near Buckingham Palace). It will be such a pleasure to have enough room to walk alongside Commodity Quay without being in danger from people coming the other way, as the passage will soon be twice as wide as before. The consensus feeling seems to be that, so far, these improvements are positive and appreciated, particularly bearing in mind the depth of current economic problems. We look forward to the new retail and catering outlets on the way and it is hoped that good communication will continue and develop further to everyone's satisfaction. On a historical note, the current owners are known to have access to experience and great expertise in this field, and it will not be surprising if they have certain plans to unfold further in this direction, which are likely to be of great benefit.

Friends of St Katharine Docks

This organisation was originally formed to fend off a previous scheme for development, which most people were unhappy about. They were successful in this, and have now evolved into a more social orientated association, while gently keeping a weather eye on what is going on. Some might wish that it had been organised back in the 1980s, when plans were being considered for an underground station here; it may well have succeeded in persuading the authorities at the time. There are weekly coffee mornings and inexpensive monthly gatherings at different, interesting venues. Membership cost is affordable, and soon recouped by using the generous discounts offered by most of the cafes, restaurants and other businesses in the Docks. Anyone can join and there are more details on the FOSKD website, listed at the end of the book.

CHAPTER SEVEN

Locations of The Docks

———◄○►———

Tower Bridge

London Bridge had been hopelessly over used for many years, without resolution. Finally, in 1876, the City of London Corporation grasped the nettle and put out tenders for the building of a new bridge east of London Bridge. More than fifty plans were put forward, and it took until 1884 for the final design to be agreed, won by Horace Jones (City architect) and John Wolfe Barry (civil engineer).

Tower Bridge 1900

Horace Jones (1819–1887), Architect

The 'bascule' (French for seesaw) bridge took eight years to build and was opened in 1892 by the Prince of Wales. Five major contractors and more than 400 workers were involved. 70000 tons of concrete were sunk into the riverbed for foundations and more than 11000 tons of steel were used for the towers and walkway framework. This was then clad in Portland Stone and Cornish granite, which protected the steelwork and gave its magnificent Gothic appearance. The bascules are raised and lowered by a hydraulic system, which powers the huge pumping engines using steam. Unfortunately, architect Jones, who had also designed Billingsgate, Leadenhall and Smithfield Markets, and was knighted in 1886, died soon after building commenced, so the extra strain was successfully carried by engineer Barry, who was knighted in 1887 and was responsible for Cannon Street Railway Bridge, Blackfriars Railway Bridge and Kew Bridge. Incidentally, Tower Subway was built in 1870 and was the world's first underground railway – it was converted as a pedestrian tunnel after only three months, relying on toll payments for income. When Tower Bridge opened, it was free for pedestrians, so the tunnel was forced to close in 1898.

Tower Hotel

Often criticised for its 'rugged exterior', it may be helpful to recall that, at the time, the Royal Festival Hall and the Barbican were being hailed as modern and progressive; money was in short supply as the UK was still recovering from the war years and vast amounts of planning and investment were necessary to repair the damage. Importantly, there was an idea to blend the hotel with the nearby Tower, Bridge and particularly with the original austere grey drabness of the Telford/Hardwick 1828 warehouses. The building was also designed to be washed every five years, which was never achieved, while the windows were deliberately designed to imitate modern ship windows. Peter Bird, the well respected J Lyons historian, has agreed for this abridged version of his description to be taken from his book, 'The First Food Empire: A History of J. Lyons & Co':

First Day Cover

The First Food Empire: A History of J.Lyons & Co, Peter Bird

'The Tower Hotel was opened by Field Marshall Sir Richard Hull GCB, DSO Constable of the Tower of London, on 19 September 1973. A band of the Grenadier Guards greeted guests arriving for the opening luncheon, which was televised by BBC Television. Most new hotel development post WWII had been to the west of London, particularly along the Cromwell Road and out towards Heathrow Airport, indeed Lyons themselves opened their Ariel Hotel in 1961 close to Heathrow Airport. The Tower Hotel was the largest hotel development of the twentieth century east of the City of London. It took three years to build on a very difficult island site in the historic area of London known as St Katharine's Dock. Without doubt, the Tower Hotel enjoys the finest location of any hotel in London, with magnificent views across Tower Bridge and the river. On the opposite side of the river bank is Butler's Wharf, where, in its earlier days, Lyons had their tea warehouses. A feature of the hotel were the high volume pumps which had been installed in the basement area in case of flooding by the Thames. This was before the Thames Barrier had been built downstream at Greenwich. The hotel had 860 bedrooms, three restaurants, a bar, banqueting suites and penthouse suites arranged on fourteen floors. The rooms had a ship's cabin quality appropriate to a riverside setting, emphasised by the nautical detailing on the furniture, bathroom interiors and compact storage facilities. The main restaurant was the 108 seat Princess Room with its own cocktail lounge and views of the river and Tower Bridge. Live music was played by a series of ensembles with a harpist being one of the favourites. The Carvery (an innovation introduced earlier in some of the company's hotels, from America) was in contrast in brilliant reds to reflect the meat being served off the bone. A fixed price of £2.20 covered a complete meal and service with an 'eat as much as you like' value. The decline in the fortunes of Lyons in the mid 1970s triggered the sale of their hotels, most of which were sold to the Charles Forte Group. The Tower Hotel, however, was sold to EMI in July 1977.'

Tower Hotel   *Guoman Hotel window*

Although a major renovation programme has at last been agreed to finally improve the exterior of the hotel, it has been allowed to deteriorate for far too many years. The Tower Hotel can proudly boast a prestigious location and neighbouring buildings, yet its exterior upkeep has been disgracefully neglected.

The Dickens Inn

This historic building has a fascinating history. The original structure was a timber framed warehouse, which was built in the 1700s and stood some distance eastwards, probably on ground now occupied by Mews Street. It escaped destruction when the new Docks were being built in the late 1820s, and was encased with an outer brick shell to conform with the other warehouses being constructed at that time. Despite the damage to the East Dock during the Blitz, the old warehouse survived, before being scheduled for demolition in the early 70s to make way for the building of housing as part of the new yacht haven redevelopment. Once the historical timber frame was discovered, the bricks were discarded and a decision was made to move it approximately seventy metres, to its present site, to become the framework for today's Dickens Inn. This

*Eighteenth century warehouse frame used in the building
of the Dickens Inn*

shell weighed 120 tons and needed expert attention during the move, which was achieved by rollers and witnessed by a very excited crowd – the rollers were described by one onlooker as 'dolls eyes'. When in position, the restoration was completed in the style of an eighteenth century inn, with three storeys and balconies on each floor. There is an interesting photograph display of this period in the entrance foyer.

Although Charles Dickens had nothing to do with this building, it may be noted that he was probably familiar with both the original warehouse and the current site. Dickens' Uncle Huffam lived at Limehouse, where the boy visited as a child; even then he was known to have been a good walker, so may not have been able to avoid the allure of The Tower of London and nearby St Katharine's Hospital and Precinct. He featured the work of lightermen in 'Our Mutual Friend' and only ten minutes walk north eastwards is the area around St George In The East where the opium den and its infamous madame, Princess Puffer, were featured in Dickens' last novel, 'The Mystery of Edwin Drood', while various of his characters came from Tower Hill and nearby. The inn was formally opened by Cedric Charles Dickens (grandson of the great

The Dickens Inn

man), who said, 'My great grandfather would have loved this inn'. The place attracts large numbers, and a tribute must be paid to their year round floral display, which is always breath taking and adds to the overall attraction of the Docks.

'Charles Dickens and a Tiny Tim' by Jane Young

International House

Stretching elegantly along the breadth of the West Dock, the nine-storey commercial building was built in the late 1970s in the style of the earlier Telford/Hardwick warehouses it replaced, featuring an imposing colonnade of original hollow cast-iron Tuscan columns salvaged from one of the Phillip Hardwick warehouses. There had been some opposition to the demolition of the remaining warehouses and a mysterious fire in 1973 did a great deal of damage. The current owners have greatly improved access by building a pontoon walkway along the whole length of its frontage and opening a prominent 'front entrance' to the dock, this allows the public to walk at water level, appreciating the Thames barges which are usually moored there, with the Tuscan columns towering above creating a real sense of history.

International House

Tower Bridge House

Tower Bridge House

This glass covered building was built to replace Europe House (1964), which was the last building to have been built during the working dockyard days and was not considered high enough in standard or impressive enough for such a prestigious position, opposite the Tower of London and so close to Tower Bridge.

Europe House had become the headquarters for London's World Trade Centre. The concept was to attract international business clients and residents; its model was the 'twin towers' complex in New York, then under construction. Peter Drew was deeply interested in global trade links and eventually the Guild of World Traders was formed in 1985, with Drew serving as its first Master. Livery status followed in January 2000.

Commodity Quay

Forming the north side wall of the West Dock, Commodity Quay was constructed in 1985 and is a six storey commercial

Commodity Quay

development, also in the style of the original warehouses. It also has access from East Smithfield and the original Telford Dock walls were retained and preserved with a grade 2 listing. Built to house the London Commodity Exchange and incorporating two trading floors, great past names such as London Fox, Liffe's and International Petroleum traded here, with in excess of 2000 traders working in its heyday. Unfortunately, by 2000 business had deteriorated so much that the trading floors had to cease operations; those remaining having to find employment in other locations. This was also the London Office for Reuters. There have been various criticisms of the building – one is its unexciting frontage and narrow walkway for pedestrians, which is now being addressed.

Marble Quay

Built in the 1980s, this distinctive three-storey 'Dutch' gabled building accommodates a restaurant, offices and character flats.

Devon House

The five-storey commercial development completed in 1987 was originally for the Port of London Authority, who are now based at Gravesend. It fronts onto the Thames and has free access to the river for the public. One of the tenants is the Alzheimer's Society, the UK's leading support and research charity for people with dementia, their families and carers.

Coronarium

This was built in 1977 to commemorate the Queen's Silver Jubilee and act as an all faith chapel. The site at the entrance to West Dock from the Central Basin was chosen as the nearest available to the actual site of the ancient Royal Hospital and Church (built in 1148 and demolished in 1825 to make way for the Telford Dock); as a serious attempt to recognise the previous religious importance in the area. Dedicated in 1977, the attractive, round, mainly glass building was designed by Hurden, Gill and Dent, and incorporated seven of the original 1828 Tuscan columns. Simply furnished inside, there was an alter, a wooden carving of Lazarus, a font fashioned from a stone taken from the original site and two wrought iron candlesticks. For many years it served for baptisms, weddings and other special services, including an annual commemoration of St Katharine, on her Saints Day, November 25th; some of these events were serviced by clergy from nearby All Hallows by the Tower and broadcast around the area by loudspeaker. Regrettably, demand was eventually considered insufficient to retain the

Coronarium

chapel, so the building was reopened as a coffee bar and eventually sold to Starbucks, the current owner.

Starbucks have made a positive contribution to the property by exhibiting an interesting tableau of the old working Docks in several of the windows. They also agreed to remove a large illuminated sign when it was considered to be out of keeping when viewed from a distance. The manager has said that he is proud to be able to tell customers and friends that his branch is the only one in the world to have a welcome from Her Majesty, Queen Elizabeth II.

Crystal Crown

The sculpture by Arthur Fleischmann was previously placed across the entrance to the Coronarium, and is now high on the wall close by. It was unveiled by H.M. Queen Elizabeth II when she visited the Coronarium in 1977.

The acrylic block, at two tons, the largest ever cast, had originally been commissioned by Stanley Kubrick, to be an alien monolith for the film '2001, A Space Odyssey'; but he rejected it for black basalt. To fashion the glittering sculpture,

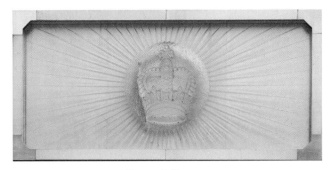

Crystal Crown

the well-known Slovak sculptor, noted for his work in Perspex worked patiently for three months in a polythene tent on the quay, close to the Coronarium. Though illuminated at night, it would be restored to full advantage if it could one day benefit from another position where it can be seen with daylight behind it, to allow it to sparkle once again.

Coronarium Bridge

This attractive, wooden, Dutch-styled bridge was built in 1983 to improve pedestrian access around the Docks.

City Quay

The northern and eastern sides of East Dock are now dominated by more than two hundred private flats, designed

City Quay

for Taylor Woodrow by Norman and Dawburn and built between 1995–7 'to reflect the character of the early nineteenth century warehouses in a contemporary way'. Built on six storeys, they also have two and three storey penthouses, which extend above the roof level. They mimic the original warehouses by having arcades of Tuscan columns (though not the originals) rising two storeys. The views over the Marina and across to Tower Bridge are, of course, stunning.

South Quay

Taylor Woodrow agreed to provide social housing as part of the contract with the GLC. South Quay was built in a modernist style, with levels varying from four to eight storeys, mainly in red brick with wood-cladding at higher levels. A network of elevated walkways links communal courtyards and the estate benefits from mature trees and other garden features; Cloysters Green and Maudlins Green are particularly attractive and the estate is largely peaceful and quite secluded.

The GLC (Conservative at the time) established the development on a 'higher rent' basis, which meant that those applying to be initial residents had to meet certain new criteria. This included no children, no animals, employment either within Tower Hamlets or the City Of London, and they had to produce proof of income. A main aim was to provide a place where young City workers on lower pay could afford to live close to where they worked – helping to resolve a specific shortage identified by City employers and politicians. The first group of residents therefore contained a particularly high proportion of what might generally be known as 'young professionals', although it also included many middle-aged and older individuals or couples. The GLC initially blocked the launch of the Right To Buy scheme under the Thatcher government in South Quay, although this changed with their demise, when ownership passed to Tower Hamlets Borough Council. With Right to Buy, like many other social housing initiatives close to the City, the composition of tenants in

South Quay Estate changed significantly during the 1980s and 1990s. As a result, a significant proportion of the Estate's 300 flats were transferred into private ownership. This transfer from public to private housing was completed in 2007 when most of the property owners purchased the freehold for the Estate from the Tower Hamlets Borough Council.

Thomas More Street

This street is the eastern boundary of St Katharine's and was the western boundary of the London Docks. Sir Thomas More was the great Chancellor of England, eventually beheaded at the Tower. Originally, it was called Nightingale Lane and was infamously renowned for being the home of many of the worst London villains down the centuries. It achieved fame again recently when the 'press brigade' gathered month after month to get pictures and interviews from News International executives and staff as they crossed the road during the phone tapping scandal.

Sir Thomas More

Ivory House at night

Ivory House

Built in 1852, this marvellous building survived bombing during the war and is the only remaining warehouse from the Telford era. By 1969 it had become derelict and so was restored in 1973. Taylor Woodrow put in a mezzanine floor and strengthened the structure of the building by using reinforced concrete. The broken clock was repaired and the bell, nearby, now chimes the hour instead of being used to call the dockers for work. Previously attracting short lets, it now has thirty-six flats for permanent use. It had housed the offices of St Katharine by the Tower Ltd and is still the headquarters of architects RHWL, who worked on the developments for Taylor Woodrow, including the renovation of Ivory House.

Tower Walk

On the south side of the Central Basin, this crescent shaped building was developed by Taylor Woodrow to commemorate the moving of the Royal Foundation of St Katharine to Regents Park in 1826. In the style of Nash, it contains seven luxury residences on three storeys over a lower ground floor. Stones from the original Docks are featured in the garden, and

Tower Walk

original Tuscan Columns from Hardwick's 1828 warehouses emphasise the classical design. On the wall facing Devon House, a new 'wall garden' has been added; much admired by people passing, again using original dock stone.

Mews Street

Situated on the south quay in East Dock, these attractive, picturesque homes were previously known as Quay Cottages. They add a contrasting style to the area.

Mews Cottages

Kilikya's Restaurant

Shops, Cafes and Restaurants

As interest in the Docks has grown, more traders have been attracted to the area and we are gradually being spoiled for choice. It is noticeable that more pedestrians pass through on their way to and from Wapping and many more visitors are being attracted, both on a frequent basis and for the 'special events' which are being presented. Some people living in the area express anxiety about noise, and it would be a great shame if it became a more serious problem. The owner of Kilikya's Restaurant has been very conscious of this and has invested in extensive soundproofing and odour filtration systems. Security staff are successful in stopping cycling within the Docks. There are other similar examples of good planning and it is hoped that licenses can be strictly controlled and monitored, so that common sense prevails and everyone can enjoy these facilities.

The Alexander Miles Gallery Ltd

Overlooking the Central Basin, close to Starbucks and The Coronarium Bridge, is where Alex is located. He is passionate about both the artists he supports and the Docks in which he works. He recently raised £10000 for the Alzheimer's Society (also based here, at Devon House).

Matilda House

This building is just outside the Docks perimeter, on St Katharine's Way, but is right to include because of its historical name. It survived the Blitz, though proud claims were made of shrapnel marks, still on some of the walls. There is also an established theory that it was deliberately not bombed by the Luftwaffe, as it offered a recognisable landmark, easily seen from the air. A plaque shows that it was the first ever 'Coop' and was only recently returned to Tower Hamlets as landlord. It also has a very fine collection of trees.

Matilda House plaque

CHAPTER EIGHT

Some of the Noted Vessels in The Docks

———◄◦►———

Gloriana

Her Majesty the Queen named the Royal Rowbarge *Gloriana* as a lasting legacy to mark her Diamond Jubilee. Her Majesty has asked that *Gloriana* be retained by Lord Sterling, who built and financed the vessel and the Maritime Heritage Trust with assistance from Thames Alive, and has approved the principle that the boat will be used to better promote the Thames. This can be achieved through providing opportunities for Royal-supported charities, and others, to play their part in occasions and celebrations upon the Thames, with a particular emphasis on events involving young people.

How wonderful to see the *Gloriana*, moored here at her permanent home when not being used elsewhere. The million pound rowbarge, painstakingly hand built over more than four years by sixty craftsmen, was certainly one of the main attractions in the recent Thames Diamond Jubilee Pageant, leading more than 1,000 boats to honour the occasion. The first royal barge to be built in 100 years, *Gloriana* was powered on the day by eighteen oarsmen, led by Britain's greatest Olympian, Sir Steve Redgrave.

Lady Daphne

(One of six Thames Barges berthed here)

Sailing Barge Lady Daphne was commissioned in 1921 to be built by Short Bros on behalf of David and Stanley Bradley of Thomas Watson (Shipping), who had a tradition of naming vessels prefaced by 'Lady'. When the barge was launched in 1923, David named it after his newly born first child, Daphne. The Lady Daphne transferred to David's wife, Lillian Bradley, on his death in 1928 and Lillian sold her to R&W Paul, the

Lady Daphne leaving St Katharine Docks

maltsters, in 1937. Thomas Watson ultimately owned 55 sailing barges and 39 coasters along the Medway and Thames, before the firm closed in 2000. While technically going through a number of R&W Paul companies, Lady Daphne was with the maltsters until her sale to Taylor Woodrow and St Katharine's Yacht Haven in 1973. In 1996 Lady Daphne was sold to Elisabeth and Michael Mainelli, who are raising funds through charter to maintain and restore her to her original condition.

'She was known as the "Lucky Lady Daphne" for an extraordinary incident. On Boxing Day 1927 the skipper was washed overboard and two crew abandoned her off the Cornish coast, but Lady Daphne, guided by the skipper's canary, sailed herself through the rocks of the Scilly Isles onto a few tens of yards of safe sand. In the 1920s she also acquired a reputation as "the fastest barge in the three channels". Lady Daphne has since been associated for a quarter of a century with the redevelopment of St Katharine's by the Tower and is a famous London fixture – the Queen Mother has visited her; numerous articles have covered her sailing ability and she has appeared in plenty of film and television shows.

The Lady Daphne Shrimper Trophy is awarded annually to the shrimper owner showing outstanding seamanship. It was first awarded as a mark of respect by Lady Daphne in the early 1980s, when she accompanied four shrimpers down to Cornwall after Cowes Week. The Shrimper Owners Association publicises the awards in its magazine, which is sent each quarter to all Shrimper Association members (circa 500 of the 850 boats built).

Flamant Rose

Nestling in the tranquil waters of East Dock is Edith Piaf's love boat. The Flamant Rose has a stylish though gentile dignity, masking a stunningly opulent and charismatic interior. James and Valerie are the proud owners, who lovingly care for it and keep it in excellent order. They both have their own depth of personality, yet successfully preserve Piaf's charisma and dynamism throughout. When James first saw the boat, he says it was love at first sight; when he told his wife, Valerie, that he was buying it, she recalls being stunned and amazed.

Flamant Rose interior

Flamant Rose

Flamant Rose exterior

Flamant Rose (or Pink Flamingo) was previously moored on the Seine in Paris, and was Piaf's base when on tour – though the public would be told that she was staying at the best local hotel. The French boxer Marcel Cerdan would have been one of the boats most cherished visitors. Piaf's short but all-consuming affair with the great sportsman ended in tragedy with his accidental death while travelling to see her in America. Though she sang the song *Je Ne Regrette Rien* (I have no regrets) shortly after this, in truth, she never fully recovered.

Havengore

Specially commissioned by the Port of London Authority in 1954 to act both as its flagship and principal survey vessel, Havengore was constructed to the highest standards of British craftsmanship using English oak and teak. Completely restored between 1997 and 2008, this distinguished vessel has now resumed her former role and continues to take part in ceremonial occasions and the hosting of visiting dignitaries.

Havengore

Havengore's proudest moment so far came in 1965 when, watched live by a worldwide audience of 350 million, she took centre stage as she carried Sir Winston Churchill on his final journey by water along the Thames. "And so Havengore sails into history – not even the Golden Hind has borne so great a man." Richard Dimbleby, BBC Lead Commentator, 30th January 1965.

On 17th May 2012 it was announced that the Havengore had been selected to carry members of the royal family as part of Queen Elizabeth II's Diamond Jubilee celebrations, in a flotilla of over a thousand vessels during the River Thames pageant on 3rd June 2012.

Aft deck of Havengore, used to carry Winston Churchill's coffin during his state funeral

CHAPTER NINE

Reflections on The Docks

—◀◦▶—

The Tenants

Some of the earlier tenants of South Quay, though very pleased overall, agree that care and standards suffered when Tower Hamlets took over the properties from the GLC, and there was a sense that the council regarded them as very lucky to have such a pleasant location, leading some tenants to feel neglected by comparison to those in other properties in the area. There was also controversy about the unfair two tier rent system and some of the flats were considered smaller than originally planned.

Liz Robinson

Liz Robinson was particularly delighted to move into South Quay, having previously had to trudge up and down seventeen flights of stairs at her flat in Woolwich, and recalls being given a substantial welcome basket by the management company, St Katharine by the Tower. Her favourite restaurant was The Warehouse (now Devonshire House), but for her, the Yacht Club was the hub of the area, which she often visited. Another favourite was the Captain's Cabin, the pub at the Dock gates. Coincidentally, as a youngster Liz went to Sunday School at St Paul's, Shadwell, where, in 1948, it merged with St James in Butcher Row and became the new home of The Royal Foundation of St Katharine, which still thrives today (as discussed elsewhere in the book).

Rita Lewis also loves living here, but has some very astute recollections of some of the earlier rules and regulations. She and others have pointed out that, originally, South Quay was scheduled to be closer to East Dock, with better views, but the plans were amended to allow Mews Cottages to be built. She regrets that so many of the shops have been replaced by cafes

Rita Lewis

and coffee shops and misses the community events that used to take place, but she produced some fascinating photos of the African Queen (from the famous C.S. Forrester story), which visited St Katharine's, as well as several others, which made an interesting display at the recent exhibition, 'Celebrating St Katharine's'. Rita recalls passing outside the Docks as a child and asking her mother what was behind the great, high walls. She also vividly remembers that the Thames was very dirty. Interestingly, Rita and her husband moved in during the 1980s, encouraged by a scheme operated by the Council; their family was grown up, so they gave up a bigger flat, releasing much needed social housing bedrooms, in favour of smaller accommodation at South Quay, and in return were given £500 to help with the move.

Brian Pietrzybav recalls that when he had a small boat in the Docks, Dockmaster Robin Knox-Johnston helped him with a problem on the keel. When he questioned Robin as to why he was putting many tins of food onto his own boat, Knox-Johnston relayed that he was storing them ready for his voyage around the world!

Sheila Reed is another content older resident. A favourite memory for her was celebrating the Queen Mother's eightieth birthday. There was a special party, which her four-year-old daughter

Brian Pietrzybav

Sheila Reed

thought was for her, as she shared the same birthdate. Sheila chaired the St Katharine's Community Association at one stage and took a great interest in local resident events. The view from her flat was wonderful in the early days, because she could look right across to the Yacht Club and watch the tops of cranes loading and unloading on the river, but this was unfortunately spoiled by new flats being built.

Elsie Cayley worked at the Tower Hotel as a waitress in The Carvery Restaurant from its opening until her retirement in 1983. She had previously worked at the Lyons Corner House in the Strand, so was probably chosen specially to join the opening team. In those days, most of the senior executives in the J Lyons 'family' were Salmons, Josephs and Glucksteins and they were justly proud of their new flagship hotel opening on the prestigious site. She often mentioned the stars and personalities she had served and talked to, including John Wayne, Miss World, John Thaw and Dennis Waterman. She was very proud of the Hotel and the Docks, and talked of seeing many changes over the years.

Elsie Cayley would have been proud of the famous Lyons uniform

Terry Cayley

Another Cayley to arrive at the Tower Hotel was son **Terry** in 1982, starting as a luggage porter and gradually gaining experience and promotion, becoming Head Porter at the young age of 23, a position he still holds today, though now referred to as Head Concierge. Terry has many memories of the Docks himself – he recalls childhood, when he could walk through a tunnel from

94

Shadwell to News International, and how he loved looking at the Nore Lightship and Captain Scott's Discovery, once moored here. One of his adult favourites was the Warehouse Restaurant, next to the Harbour Master's House (now Devon House), where he had great times with other staff and locals. Many of the other staff in those early days had been dockers, so he heard many great stories about what life had been like in the past. The centenary of Tower Bridge was a marvellous highlight for him, and Royal Yacht Britannia was a splendid sight, moored at St Katharine Pier shortly before decommissioning.

Tony Cayley, who works alongside his older brother as Deputy Head Concierge, well remembers seeing the Queen opening the Coronarium in 1977, standing in front of John Harding's hairdressing salon with mother Elsie and sister Linda: "I felt very proud and patriotic. It was like the Jubilee, packed with people, the Queen looked wonderful and we could all hear the ceremony on loudspeakers." Another favourite for him

Tony Cayley

was the collection of tall ships that gathered along the Thames and in St Katharine Docks in the late eighties – he says that the whole river seemed full of these beautiful ships, a reminder of what all the tea clippers and traders must have looked like, waiting to put their cargoes ashore. As a child, his first memory was of the red bridge, from the lock into the Central Basin, while an early recollection of the East Dock was that much of it was an open car park. Though the remaining docks were rundown, he didn't think of them as derelict, as there were always lots of boats and barges, and so many other exciting things to see. Their mother was devastated to hear that the world famous Lyons Carvery at the Tower was to close, as the establishments were an institutional part of London in their day (others, at The Cumberland and Regent Palace have also closed, though the one at The Strand Palace still thrives). Sadly,

Elsie passed away recently, interestingly within days of the Carvery closing.

Fiona Harding

Fiona Harding arrived at St Katharine's in September 1987, to take over the hairdresser's shop near Coronarium Bridge, next to Zizzi's. The hairdresser's had previously been run by Jennifer Drew, daughter of Peter Drew, who developed the modern Docks for Taylor Woodrow. Fiona has very pleasant memories of the Docks, not least when recalling the Coronarium; she says that it was a very imposing building – plain, with glass between the pillars – while inside there was an alter and just one statue. The clergy were very accommodating and enthusiastic, one of whom used to come in for a haircut and beard trim. Fiona remembers the Docks being very different in days passed – the Lightship restaurant was berthed close by, there was a nursery and fruit and veg shop on the river front, before Devon House was built, and it was very convenient having both NatWest and Midland Bank in the World Traders building (now Commodity Quay). The very lively Yacht Club was next door, before it became a restaurant, and her neighbour on the other side was a smart gift shop which sold crystal glass, Wedgewood and similar, and attracted a lot of Americans staying at the Hotel. She recalls traders from the London Fox in Commodities House (Futures and Options Exchange, who traded in commodities) with their distinctive jackets and outgoing, pleasant personalities, bustling around at lunchtimes, looking for places to eat. Fiona used to cut Peter Drew's hair (she referred to him as 'the big boss') and remembers him as very charismatic, charming and polite. However, she was extremely upset when the famous footballer and manager Kevin Keegan turned up without an appointment, because she was too busy and had to turn him away. Fiona's father John, who joined her after ten years, is also a well-known and loved character at St Katharine's. Vidal Sassoon (who hailed from nearby Whitechapel) was a great influence on John, who went to his very first demo at a hotel in Knightsbridge when he was sixteen. John formed the 'London Hair Fashion Group', which aimed to improve standards of members and was quite a trend-setting influence. He remembers numerous celebrity clients, including Peter Sellers, Tony Curtis and Vanessa, Michael and Lynn Redgrave. The best times for him, looking back, was when Taylor Woodrow were landlords: 'They were very under-standing, worked hard for the place and it was a real community in those days.'

Ron Aspinall has worked at the Docks since June 1989, seeing a great many changes and modernisations. He was taken on as lockkeeper by Peter Drew, and is very happy about the time spent there, recalling Drew with great respect. Ron also worked well with Sir Robin Knox-Johnston, the first person to sail around the world single-handed without stopping, and says that he had many great ideas and always led from the front, doing many of the most difficult jobs himself. Sir Robin inspired him because he would always encourage people to have a go, saying, 'try it, it doesn't matter if it doesn't work'. Ron's favourite memory is of the Tall Ships that gathered to race in the early 90s; he recalls the incredible spectacle of the Docks jammed full with these ships from all around the world, the crews wearing naval type uniforms. The bigger ships were moored out in the Thames and the sight was unforgettable across the river, while the atmosphere was fantastic, with everyone excited and getting on well with each other. Each evening there were parties, food and fireworks, and many friendships were made, before a huge anticlimax once the ships had left. Similarly, there were great celebrations for the Jubilee and the new Millennium. Ron was deeply shocked when Taylor Woodrow sold, as the Docks had been a family, growing together. He doesn't rate the several past owners nearly as well, though is very buoyant about the current owners and thinks they are the best yet. He feels very strongly that they are providing the best equipment, including the new pontoons, and there is more freedom to allow the professionals to get on with the job without being constrained by too much caution and control (as was particularly the case in the Taylor Woodrow days) – one important outcome of this is that they can get the boats in much quicker. Ron loves his work and is enthusiastic, looking forward to the future.

Sara Biddle says, 'I am so fortunate to live and work around St Katharine's. I love the variety and the depth of history, with the newness of some buildings complimenting the old ones. It's unique, quaint and quiet, a place to let your imagination skip back in time, on the doorstep of our great City. I love the boats and barges visiting, they keep it fluid, ever reminding me of a different pace  and way of life. It feels extra special now, having the grand presence of the Royal barge Gloriana. Gorgeous golden sunshine, even on our greyest of days.'

Rev Mark Aitken

Rev Mark Aitken, Master, Royal Foundation of St Katharine, Limehouse from a discussion soon after his appointment

'My first thought on the historical aspect of the appointment, is a real sense of standing in an amazingly long succession of Masters. There are very few other appointments that put you into such a chain of characters and also such a group of people to have survived through such historical changes. So I am very aware of the historical dimension as current Master of St Katharine's, which adds an interesting dimension to the role. There is a need to balance the requirements of what needs to be done for the people here during the day, while taking a long-term perspective about what actually is the long-term objective of this organisation. Having survived for such a long time, what is the appropriate way forward in our current, fast moving world? Several of the people sitting on the managing court here work in similar organisations which have long term perspectives; one is responsible for managing the fabric of Westminster Abbey, another works for the Royal family, yet another is the Bishop of London. There is an overall sense of importance about holding and preserving the aims for which St Katharine's was created.

The lineage of Masters is among the oldest known, historically, with a current vibrancy of activity which has adapted and changed while holding onto its roots. Links are developing with St Katharine Docks; the recent visits by the Friends of St Katharine Docks, other residents and boat owners has developed some closeness with the permanent community, already which also helps us to remember our roots. This book is also a useful link and we are not far away, geographically.

Whether the Hospital and Church should have been razed to the ground in the 1820s is a difficult question. Commenting on historical matters is not my natural field, but being a geographer I am interested in the way areas change. It was obviously a hugely controversial action at the time, and was caught up in the wider political issues, as was the Church. It is curious that the clergy were able to find a new home in Regents Park with increased resources, and the Church, perhaps, didn't behave in a way that one could be proud of. It's difficult to know, in hindsight, what would have happened if it had continued. I'm delighted to be living here, at nearby Limehouse, and I'm absolutely thrilled that St Katharine's has survived through this period of time. If we had stayed where we were, might we have been consumed at a later period by a big new development and just disappeared? This would have been a great shame. So the great thing is that St Katharine's has survived, but we have also lost a whole community or village, which was just destroyed!

I do get very excited about the relics here – it is delightful to see historians clambering over the stalls and admiring the misericords and we are now getting more walking tours and historical organisations visiting us. There is a sense that we are opening ourselves up to sharing these treasures, many of which are still in excellent condition, with some of them still in regular use. There is an interesting sweep of history within the chapel; these fascinating works have been with us and travelled with us through the ages and now their roots are laid down here. There are modern aspects, such as the alter, which was built specially for here, which I think work well together – some others disagree, but I think it's done very well. It's an easy place for people to come and be at peace. We are currently taking steps to inform historical agencies and others about what is here. We are also looking at ways to further display historical documents and other items, some of which are elsewhere and we are in the process of getting them back.'

Wendy Taylor CBE

A most important figure locally (and, of course, nationally), Wendy Taylor loves the Docks and has been influential in its development and growth. In the book written about her, Edward Lucie-Smith says, 'She is unique because of the nature of her work – and also because of its wide dissemination and the frequency with which the public comes in

'Timepiece'

contact with it. The probability is that she has more major sculptures on permanent public display in Britain than any other living artist... Timepiece often appears prominently in the foreground of photographs which are meant to conjure up the image of modern London, a city rooted in tradition, but looking hopefully to the future. Significantly, however, the sculptor herself is seldom credited in the caption to the picture. Wendy Taylor's work is now so much a part of the public consciousness that her own identity often seems to be concealed, rather than revealed by the success of what she does.' Taylor also sculpted the Dove Memorial, at the nearby Hermitage Riverside Memorial Gardens. After twenty years of struggle and fund raising by dedicated local residents, the Council was persuaded to build the Gardens instead of concreting over the site of Hermitage Wharf. The Gardens were dedicated to the memory of the East End civilians who died in the Second World War, a sentiment shared in the Dove Memorial: while it represents hope, the cutaway shape of the bird symbolises the civilians who lost their lives. The sculptor donated her fee to the local resident fundraisers.

Disappointed at London not being short-listed for a competition to produce a piece of outdoor sculpture for one of six specific cities, Wendy Taylor pressed ahead with an idea for what she would have produced had she and London been selected. She lived and worked in St Katharine Docks at this time, with all its maritime associations. Her idea was for a large sundial, which would also be a contemporary sculpture. She chose common dock materials to symbolize the local area, using chains and shackles to support the sundial: the ring is a large washer and the gnomon (pointer) represents a traditional dockyard nail. This work came to the attention of directors of Strand Hotels, who were the owners of the Tower Hotel, being built close to her studio on the waterfront. They commissioned her to complete this important sculpture, ready for their opening. Incidentally, Strand Hotels was part of J Lyons and Co., who famously imported tea from across the world to their warehouses at Butlers Wharf, on the other side of the Thames, directly opposite Timepiece. In 2004 the Heritage Minister, Andrew McIntosh, declared Timepiece as a Marathon Landmark, to be protected from today. 'Because so many exist, a post-war structure needs to be of exceptional quality and character in order to qualify for listing. 'Timepiece', the well-loved landmark sculpture by Wendy Taylor, is just such an exception.'

The inscription on the stainless steel plaque at the base of sculpture says: 'The sundial is one of man's oldest astronomical instruments. In this particular form, known as an Equinoctial Sundial, the dial is in the same plane as the earth's equator and the gnomon, or rod, is parallel to the axis of the earth pointing true north. The shadow of the gnomon moving across the dial indicates the time. In summer the shadow falls on the face of the dial, in winter on the inner edge. Due to a combination of the tilt of the earth's axis and the varying speed of the earth's progress on its elliptical path around the sun the time indicated differs by several minutes from the time shown by a clock which measures mean time – an average of these variations. This sundial was designed by Wendy Taylor and commissioned by Strand Hotels Limited in March 1973.'

Girl on a dolphin by David Wynne, also on the waterfront

CHAPTER TEN

Recent Events at St Katharine's

———◁◦▷———

St Katharine Docks hosted the 2013–14 Clipper Round The World Yacht Race. The start date was September 1st and the journey covers an incredible 40000 miles around the oceans of the world, before returning to finish where it was started: the approach to Tower Bridge in July 2014. The idea of the race is to encourage amateurs from all walks of life to take part, giving them the opportunity, thrills and personal development involved in sailing around the world. This has inspired thousands of participants, as well as encouraging countless others towards sailing and sea going experience. Up to 650 crews are involved in the current race.

The founder and chairman is Sir Robin Knox-Johnston, who established the competition back in 1996. Sir Robin was born in Putney and knows the Thames well, both from his time in the Merchant and Royal Navies and as harbour master at St

Clipper Round The World Yacht Race

Sir Robin Knox-Johnston and Mayor Boris Johnson, 2013

Katharine's in the 1970s. Mayor Boris Johnson is rightly delighted about the race starting and finishing in London, and has said "Those who take part are an inspiration to us all and exhibit the very best of the human spirit ... As they battle through everything the elements can throw at them, I wish everyone on board these stunning vessels the very best of luck." However, we should also say hats off to Sir Robin, as his inspiration is incredible and worthy of deep respect.

Sir Robin Knox-Johnston (from his own pen): 'As you may have discovered, the docks never really paid commercially as an investment. We knew that the docks could not stand alone as a financial business, the costs of the lock and the rates imposed by Tower Hamlets were too high, but it provided an attraction that raised the value of the office space being developed in the old warehouses. When I came on the scene in 1975 there were some pontoons in the Central Basin, but that was all. There were four Thames Barges, but being charged at the same rate as yachts. I halved the rate, to the disgust of the accountant, but three months later we had sixteen Thames Barges, which doubled the income and made the place more attractive, and very lively as we still had barge skippers who had been in barges all their lives and had some wonderful tales. I organised relay sailing races around the docks in laser dinghies, for Olympic sailors, sailing journalists and eventually, protesting loudly, the barge skippers. Much to everyone's surprise the barge skippers won! Of course, the real objective was publicity to draw attention to the Haven's existence, which it did, and soon we were putting more pontoons in the East and West basins.

'Our main problem, however, was the distance from any sailing waters. So we "sold" the Haven as a place to bring your boat if you wanted to visit London (a bit of a problem with Tower Hamlets council who did not want people living aboard their boats!) and gave a special lower berthing rate for the winter six months when visitors stayed at home. It was to give these boat owners some fun that I organised the Valentine's Day Frostbite Race in 1976, on, of course, 14th February. Down the Thames on the ebb tide, anchor for the night at a suitable location and race back on the flood the next day. I enjoyed my time working there, and have been pleased to return regularly.'

The Queen's Visit to HMS President

On June 3rd 2012 people around the world watched as the Queen and Prince Phillip led the Thames Pageant procession of more than 1000 boats gathered to pay tribute to Her

The Queen waves to crowds in St Katharine's Way

Majesty's 60 years on the throne. After it reached Tower Bridge, Spirit Of Chartwell moored in the river, close to HMS President, to allow the Royal party to watch as the narrow boats, tugs, Dunkirk little ships, pleasure cruisers and steam boats passed by. It rained heavily and the party refused to come ashore until all the boats had passed. The picture shows The Queen waving to the gathered crowd waiting in St Katharine's Way; it also shows Prince Phillip, who was admitted to hospital shortly after.

St Katharine's Day Commemoration 2013

Rev Canon Roger Hall MBE

On Sunday 24th November 2013, numerous people from St Katharine Docks, including residents, visitors and boat owners, attended Morning Service at the Chapel Royal in the Tower of London. They were welcomed by the Tower Chaplain, Rev Roger Hall, who was in excellent form and devoted much of his sermon to commemorating St Katharine, and then the ancient Hospital and Church that was razed to the ground to make way for the building of St Katharine Docks. As he said, the last sermon at St Katharine's was held by the then Chaplain of the Tower, Rev R.R. Bailey, who himself was bitterly opposed to the closure, and used James iv. 13 as his text: "Go to now, ye that say, to-day or to-morrow we will go into such a city, and continue there a year, and buy and sell and get gain." It was very appropriate and moving to listen to today's Chaplain all these years later.

Then, on Monday 25th November (St Katharine's Day) a commemoration ceremony was held near the site of 'Old Kate', near Starbucks, in the Central Basin at the Dock. The

*Rev. Mark Aitken, Master of RFSK, Limehouse, celebrates
St Katharine's Day on the site of the ancient hospital*

current Master of the Royal Order of St Katharine at Limehouse was the special guest, who reflected on the thousands of people who had to leave their homes in the Precinct, and the sadness of losing their wonderful place of worship when the ancient Hospital was closed. Of course, the splendid Marina of today is cherished and loved, but it is right to respect the richness of the area's past history.

On 5th January 2014 the Lord Mayor of London honoured Sir Thomas More in the Chapel Royal of St Peter ad Vincula at the Tower of London. She was chief guest attending the Epiphany Carol Service, accompanied by Sheriffs and guests from the disabled charity, Livability. She wore Sir Thomas More's historic Chain of Office, allowed only for special occasions, and read one of the lessons. After the service, she paid homage to his shrine in the Crypt. I live nearby at St Katharine's and feel so privileged to be able to use the Chapel regularly; what a wonderful extra thrill it was to witness such an important historical event.

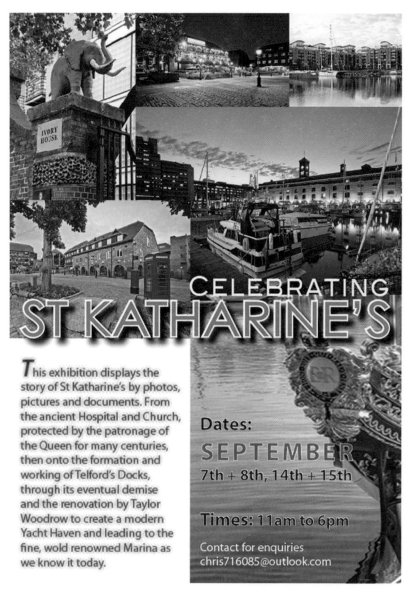

Celebrating
ST KATHARINE'S

*T*his exhibition displays the story of St Katharine's by photos, pictures and documents. From the ancient Hospital and Church, protected by the patronage of the Queen for many centuries, then onto the formation and working of Telford's Docks, through its eventual demise and the renovation by Taylor Woodrow to create a modern Yacht Haven and leading to the fine, wold renowned Marina as we know it today.

Dates:
SEPTEMBER
7th + 8th, 14th + 15th

Times: 11am to 6pm

Contact for enquiries
chris716085@outlook.com

The History of St Katharine's Exhibition 2013

During the Thames Festival, the current owners, Max Property Group Plc, generously allowed the use of a spare unit near the entrance to Ivory House for an exhibition about 'The History Of St Katharine's'; I also undertook guided tours of the Docks for interested visitors. The exhibition was very successful, with more than two thousand people passing through. The new Map and Guide of St Katharine's sold well and a great deal of interest was shown for this book, 'The Story of St Katharine's', which had not been published at that stage. Most significantly, people were intrigued to hear about the ancient Royal Hospital of St Katharine and fascinated by the richness of the more recent historical items that are exhibited within the Docks. Many expressed their surprise and delight at learning the historical importance of the area. I would like to add that it was a great excitement and pleasure to have been part of the two week Thames Festival – the collection of vintage boats gathered was the most awesome visual spectacle imaginable; watching the happiness on the faces of so many thousands was unforgettable.

Colin Mitchell, a prominent local resident, provided some of his superb photos for the exhibition, including the example below.

St Katharine's in the snow

CHAPTER ELEVEN

Tribute To Peter Drew OBE

*(Taken mainly from the Guardian and Telegraph
obituaries)*

————◄o►————

Peter Drew died, following a heart attack, on the 4th June 2007, aged 79. He was the chairman of the property and construction group Taylor Woodrow, and recognised as inspirational and pivotal towards the regeneration of the other docks in East London, following his successful redevelopment of St Katharine Docks. Born to Quaker parents in Thetford, Norfolk, in September 1927, his father worked for Fisons, the fertiliser company, until he lost his job and built up his own fishing business, which went bankrupt when Peter was only six years old. This shaped Peter's personal views in later life, making him cautious and wary about debt and business risk. Peter was an accomplished watercolour painter and he designed Taylor Woodrow's Christmas cards for many years. He was a good cook, and cherished his charming home and garden. A favourite relaxation when under pressure was boating around the Norfolk Coast – the famous sailing barge, Lady Daphne, was present to pay homage to his connection with the water at his memorial service. Drew was never afraid of difficult situations and would face them head on rather than sidestep or avoid confrontation. After school Peter studied on an Engineering course at Kingston College, then went on to Hendon College to study architecture. In 1965 he joined the property sector of Taylor Woodrow, working on planning for the St Katharine Docks project under the close eye of Frank

Plaque on a a park bench near the lock, to honour Peter Drew

(later Lord) Taylor, the legendary chairman at that time. By 1979 Drew was a member of the main board, while remaining in charge of the St Katharine's development. He was made chairman in 1989 and remained in that post until his retirement in 1992.

Drew oversaw the rebuilding of the Docks and the building of the Tower Hotel, refurbished the Ivory House warehouses into luxury flats for short lets, rebuilt extensive office accommodation, developed more than 650 private and social housing flats, moved the eighteenth century warehouse to its new position as the picturesque Dickens Inn and provided numerous outlets for cafes, restaurants and retail. He saw the area as a developing community and the Docks became his home, moving into Dockmaster's House, the house that Telford had built for himself to live and work in just below Tower Bridge. He was considered a fine business manager, being bold, energetic, flexible, imaginative and ruthless if absolutely necessary. Peter was a church warden at All Hallows by the Tower from 1972 to 1994. In 1973 he founded the World Trade Centre, London, and then became Chairman of the World Trade Centre's Association in 1974. His global interests helped to secure his OBE in 1979. He went on to establish The Guild of World Traders in 1985 and advise Margaret Thatcher's Government on the regeneration of Canary Wharf and other issues involving the Thames and East London. Other interests included being an actively involved governor of Sadlers Wells and the Museum of London and its new associate, the Docklands Museum. Peter Drew was married to Wendy Ferris, who lived with him both in the Dockmaster's House and later in Bury St Edmunds, until his death. He had a son and two daughters by previous marriage.

Without Peter Drew it is most unlikely that we would have today's
St Katharine Docks

CHAPTER TWELVE

Recent Blog Posts

---◄◦►---

Posted on 01 April 2013

*Mary Anne and Larry Leave
St Katharine Docks
For Canada*

This lively couple will be missed by many of the friends made while they berthed here at St Katharine Docks. Larry hails originally from the UK, and subsequently became an airline pilot and captain with Air Canada, while Mary Anne is Canadian, with a music teaching background.

Following retirement they watched their beloved Traversay III being built, before sailing it around the world for the past nine years. They stayed at St Katharine's for six months last year, then returned again following a cruise around Germany and Norway (where the above picture was taken). During the

Traversay III

past six months Mary Anne has had a hired clavichord on board and helped to raise £1200 for Red Nose Day; she has loved all the free music concerts and museum visits here, as well as playing baroque music with other talented artists. Larry has loved jogging as far as Shadwell Basin and lots of splendid walks around London. Not everyone has a state of the art electronic piano under the bed, but, of course, they do! They both feel deeply touched by the friendliness of the community here, particularly the Friends Of St Katharine Docks and others in the boating community. They are now returning to Canada, so bon voyage and very best wishes.

Posted on 26 June 2012

This splendid Chinese Junk will be here in St Katharine Docks until at least after the Olympics. Hua Shan is the main brains behind the venture, bringing the first Chinese vessel up the Thames for many, many years. The boat was shipped from Hong Kong to Tilbury (costing megabucks), but was apparently delayed in a queue at Suez, meaning it just missed its pride of place in the Royal Pageant celebrations. He is the father of Alexander Hua Tian, the young Chinese event equestrian, and husband of British wife Sarah Noble. Hua Shan has

Junk Huantian in St Katharine Docks

told me that they will be entertaining many of the Chinese Olympics team; with his son's strong links with horse eventing. Who knows who some of the English guests may be?

Phoenicia: On Board Exhibition at St Katharine Docks

Posted on 15 June 2012

The Phoenicia is a fascinating replica of sailing vessels dating back to 600 BC, when the Phoenicians were the world's first great maritime traders. St Katharine Docks witnessed the heights of GB as the latest great sea power, so how splendid for us to see so far back into maritime history. Captain Phillip Beale is totally dedicated and immersed in this project. His website: www.phoenicia.org.uk is very informative, with all kinds of important historical information.

CHAPTER THIRTEEN

Map and Guide Notes

—◄o►—

This is also available as a booklet, on sale via
www.historyofthedocks.com and Nauticalia

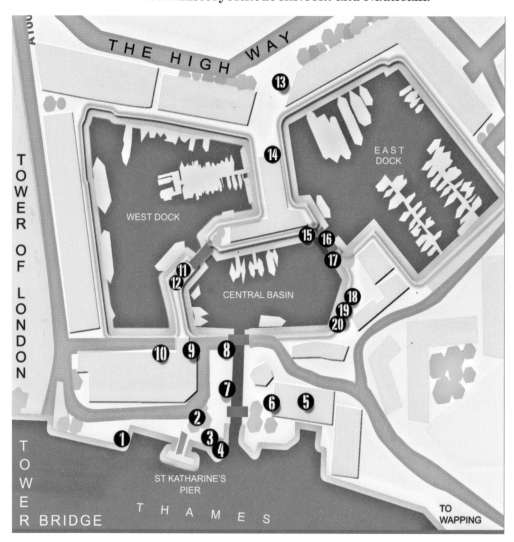

1. **Girl With A Dolphin:** (1973) Statue and fountain by David Wynne, the
famous sculptor. This work is 'sister' to *Boy with a Dolphin* (1974) in
Cheyne Walk, Chelsea. See page 102.

2. **Seat:** Commemorating Peter Drew, for his contribution to the London Walkway. The inscription reads, 'Peter Drew, OBE (1927 to 2007) who created this extension to the Jubilee Walkway. Placed here in his memory by the Trustees of the Jubilee Walkway Trust.' See page 111.

3. **'Timepiece':** Sundial Sculpture, (1973). Wendy Taylor, funded by Strand Hotels Ltd. See page 100.

4. **Cannon:** Guarding the entrance to the Docks (late seventeenth, early eighteenth century). See page 44.

5. **Dockmaster's House:** (1828) Built by Thomas Telford and architect Philip Hardwick. See page 44.

6. **King William III Plaque:** (1989) Unveiled in the presence of Queen Beatrix of the Netherlands, to commemorate three centuries of Anglo-Dutch naval friendship.

7. **Bollard:** Proudly shows St Katharine with bible, sword, wheel and nearby Tower. These are all around the Docks, carefully preserved by the Dock authorities.

8. **Here The Sea Shells:** To remember the huge tonnage of marine shells traded in the Docks. This sculpture is part of a collection by Paula Haughney, sculptor (1997 to 1999). These were commissioned originally to provide seating; made from original marble used in the early Docks and to symbolize the different cargoes which came into St Katharine Docks.

9. **Hydraulic Hoist:** These were used to load and unload the vessels in the Docks. Hydraulic power replaced steam power, which was dangerous, particularly in confined spaces.

10. **Docks Theme Enamel Panels:** Cloisters Walk: These panels vividly display aspects of work in the old Docks. Artist Dale Devereux Barker created this work in vitreous enamel, with the help of school children from four nearby schools: St Pauls Way Community School, Stepney and St Saviour's and St Olave's School, Southwark. This work was completed in 2000.

11. **Site of The Royal Hospital of St Katharine by the Tower of London:** 1148 to 1825. Prior to today's Starbucks, the building was constructed as a chapel, called The Coronarium, to celebrate the Silver Jubilee and visited by Her Majesty Queen Elizabeth II in 1977.

12. **Crystal Crown:** (1977). Hand carved by Arthur Fleischmann on this site. It is the largest block of acrylic in the world and originally stood at the entrance to the Coronarium (see 11 above). See page 79.

13. **Elephants:** (1973), Artist Peter Drew (also the 'architect' of today's splendid Marina). Made of fibreglass, representing the ivory which was such an important commodity for the Docks, hence the name of one of the converted warehouses, Ivory House. See pages 108 and 112.

14. **Marine Shells:** (1997 to 1999) By Paula Haughney, sculptor (see also '8'). Situated on each side of the entrance to Ivory House. See page 52.

15. **Echoed Aromas:** (1997 to 1999) By Paula Haughney, sculptor (see also '8'). Sofa-like structure, made with five blocks, representing vanilla, cloves, nutmeg and cinnamon.

16. **Telford's Footbridge:** (1828) Memorial to Thomas Telford, engineer (1757–1834), who built St Katharine Docks. The bridge was in use until 1994. See front cover and page 82.

17. **Anchor:** SS Amsterdam. Salvaged from the ill-fated East India merchantman, which was built in the 1740s and sank on its maiden voyage, west of Hastings. A replica of the ship is at the Royal Maritime Museum.
18. **To The Sea:** (1997 to 1999) By Paula Haughney, sculptor (see '8'). Showing a turtle to represent the large numbers of turtle and tortoise shells that were imported and used for making combs, spectacle cases and fashion accessories. See page 48.
19. **Exotic Birds:** (1997 to 1999) By Paula Haughney, sculptor (see '8'). Showing a carved bird's wing. Huge numbers of feathers were needed for ladies' hats and fans, including ostrich, peacock and osprey. See page 50.
20. **Oriental Carpet:** (1997 to 1999) By Paula Haughney, sculptor (see '8'). Representing carpets imported mainly from India, Persia and Turkey.

References

———◄◦►———

www.portcities.org.uk. Interesting insight into Dockland history

www.workersliberty.org/story/2007/10/06/tom-mann-3-%E2%80%941889-great-trade-union-turning-point-: account of life for the poor people struggling in the late 1880s.

www.historicaleye.com/dockstrike1889.html: Similar.

www.spartacus.schoolnet.co.uk/TUmatchgirls.htm: Successful strike at Bryant and May.

www.workersliberty.org/system/files/Tom%20Mann%20%E2%80%94%20his%20life%20and%20times.pdf. Authoritative account of Tom Mann.

www.clipperroundtheworld.com/ Reporting the current round the world race.

www.fundinguniverse.com/company-histories/taylor-woodrow-plc-history/: about Taylor Woodrow, who built today's St Katharine's.

www.lady-daphne.co.uk/history.html

www.wendytaylorsculpture.co.uk

www.honearchive.org/etexts/edb/daypages/303-oct30.html: Bio Text edition of The Every-Day Book, by Kyle Grimes. Account of the last service at the Royal Hospital in 1825.

www.tolpuddlemartyrs.org.uk

http://www.royall.co.uk/royall/poplar1.htm. Fine account of East End life.

http://www.british-history.ac.uk/source.aspx?pubid=593. Stow's Survey of London, also contributions by Andrew Ducarel (and many other fascinating aspects of London).

www.adachphoto.wix.com/portfolio

www.museumoflondon.org.ukdocklands/

www.foskd.org/- Friends of St Katharine Docks

www.historyofthedocks.com – Author's website

Books

The History of The Royal Hospital of St Katharine By The Tower of London, Catherine Jameson, 1952.

East London, Walter Besant, 1899.

History of the Port of London. Joseph Broodbank 1920.

East London. Robert Sinclair, Robert Hale. 1950.

The Royal Hospital or Free Chapel of St. Katharine near the Tower, c 1865.

'Couldn't Afford The Eels', Memories of Wapping 1900–1960, Martha Leigh.

Piety And Piracy, A History of Wapping And St Katharine's, Madge Darby.

Libraries

Bancroft, Tower Hamlets
Bristol
Guildhall and Barbican
Westminster
London Metropolitan Archives
The British Library

Sketch by Jane Young